The American Civil War

Sir Winston S. Churchill

The American Civil War

THE FAIRFAX PRESS

New York

ACKNOWLEDGMENTS

I desire to record my thanks again to Mr F. W. Deakin and Mr G. M. Young for their assistance before the Second World War in the preparation of this work; to Professor Asa Briggs of Leeds University, to Mr Maldwyn A. Jones of Manchester University, and to Mr Maurice Shock of University College, Oxford, who have since helped in its completion; and to Mr Alan Hodge, Mr Denis Kelly, Mr Anthony Montague Browne and Mr C. C. Wood. I have also to thank many others who have kindly read these pages and commented upon them.

For permission to include a quotation from *The Oxford History of the United States* acknowledgment is due to the Oxford University Press.

FIRST PUBLISHED IN *A History of the English Speaking Peoples: The Great Democracies,* 1958.

This 1985 edition is published by The Fairfax Press, distributed by Crown Publishers, Inc., by arrangement with Dodd, Mead, and Company, Inc.

Manufactured in the United States of America

Library of Congress Cataloging in Publication Data
Churchill, Winston, Sir, 1874–1965.
    The American Civil War.

    1. United States—History—Civil War, 1861–1865.
I. Title.
E468.C57   1985   973.7   84-26065
ISBN: 0-517-46779-8

h g f e d c b

Contents

Illustrations

The publishers wish to acknowledge the help afforded them by The Library of Congress, which with one exception provided all the photographs selected for this book. The exception is the photograph of Fort Sumter which follows page 50, supplied by the Valentine Museum, Richmond, Virginia.

ILLUSTRATIONS

Maps

The American Civil War

CHAPTER ONE

American Epic

THE year 1815 had marked the end of a period of American development. Up to this time the life of the continent had been moulded largely by forces from Europe, but with the conclusion of the war of 1812 against England America turned in upon herself and with her back to the Atlantic looked towards the West. The years following the Peace of Ghent are full of the din of the Westward advance. In politics the vehement struggles of Federalist and Republican were replaced by what a contemporary journalist called "the era of good feelings." But underneath the calm surface of the first decade lay the bitter rivalry of sectional interests which were soon to assume permanent and organised party forms. As in all post-war periods, the major political issue was that of finance. The ideas of Alexander Hamilton on Protection and banking were reluctantly accepted by the Republican administration under the stress of war conditions. The tariff of 1816 had created a régime of Protection under which New England turned from her shipping interests to manufacture and laid the foundations of her nineteenth-century prosperity. The old suspicions of Jefferson about a Federal banking system were overcome, and in 1816 a charter replacing the one which had expired was issued for the foundation of a new Federal Bank.

The ties with Europe were slowly and inexorably broken. Outstanding disputes between England and America were settled by a series of commissions. The boundaries of Canada were fixed, and both countries agreed to a mutual pact of disarmament upon that storm centre, the Great Lakes. In

1819, after straggling warfare in Spanish Florida, led by the hero of New Orleans, Andrew Jackson, the Spanish Government finally yielded the territory to the United States for five million dollars. Spain had withdrawn from the Northern continent for ever.

But the turmoils of European politics were to threaten America once again for the last time for many years to come. The sovereigns of the Old World were bound together to maintain the principle of monarchy and to co-operate in intervening in any country which showed signs of rebellion against existing institutions. The policy of this Holy Alliance had aroused the antagonism of Britain, who had refused to intervene in the internal affairs of Italy in 1821. The new crisis came in Spain. Bourbon France, burning to achieve respectability in the new Europe, sent an army across the Pyrenees to restore the Spanish monarchy. Russia would have liked to go farther. The Czar of Russia had world-wide interests, including large claims to the western coastline of North America, which he now reaffirmed by Imperial decree. Rumours also spread to Washington that the reactionary Powers of Europe, having supported the restoration of the Bourbons in Spain, might promote similar activities in the New World to restore Bourbon sovereignty there. In Southern America lay the Spanish colonies, which had in their turn thrown off the yoke of their mother country.

The British Government under Canning offered to co-operate with the United States in stopping the extension of this threatening principle of intervention to the New World. Britain announced that she recognised the sovereignty of the Latin republics in South America. Meanwhile President Monroe acted independently and issued his message to Congress proclaiming the principles later known as the Monroe Doctrine. This famous Doctrine, as has been related, was at once a

warning against interference on the part of any European
Powers in the New World and a statement of the intention of
America to play no part in European politics. With this vale-
dictory message America concentrated upon her own affairs.
A new generation of politicians was rising. The old veterans
of the days of the Constitution had most of them vanished
from the scene, though Jefferson and Madison lingered on in
graceful retirement in their Virginian homes.

*   *   *   *   *

Westward lay the march of American Empire. Within thirty
years of the establishment of the Union nine new states had
been formed in the Mississippi valley, and two in the borders
of New England. As early as 1769 men like Daniel Boone had
pushed their way into the Kentucky country, skirmishing with
the Indians. But the main movement over the mountains began during the War of Independence. The migration of the
eighteenth century took two directions: the advance westward
towards the Ohio, with its settlement of Kentucky and Tennessee, and the occupation of the north-west forest regions, the
fur-traders' domain, beyond Lake Erie. The colonisation of
New England and the eastern coastline of America had been
mainly the work of powerful companies, aided by the English
Crown or by feudal proprietors with chartered rights. But
here in the new lands of the West any man with an axe and
a rifle could carve for himself a rude frontier home. By 1790
there were thirty-five thousand settlers in the Tennessee country, and double that number in Kentucky. By 1800 there
were a million Americans west of the mountain ranges of the
Alleghenies. From these new lands a strong, self-reliant Western breed took its place in American life. Modern American
democracy was born and cradled in the valley of the Mississippi. The foresight of the first independent Congress of the
United States had proclaimed for all time the principle that

when new territories gained a certain population they should be admitted to statehood upon an equality with the existing partners of the Union. It is a proof of the quality and power of the Westerners that eleven of the eighteen Presidents of the United States between 1828 and 1901 were either born or passed the greater part of their lives in the valley of the Mississippi. Well might Daniel Webster upon an anniversary of the landing of the Pilgrim Fathers declaim the celebrated passage: "New England farms, houses, villages, and churches spread over and adorn the immense extent from the Ohio to Lake Erie and stretch along from the Alleghanies [*sic*] onwards beyond the Miamis and towards the falls of St Anthony. Two thousand miles westward from the Rock where their fathers landed may now be seen the sons of pilgrims cultivating smiling fields, rearing towns and villages, and cherishing, we trust, the patrimonial blessings of wise institutions, of liberty and religion. . . . Ere long the sons of the pilgrims will be upon the shores of the Pacific."

America was swelling rapidly in numbers as well as in area. Between 1790 and 1820 the population increased from four to nine and a half millions. Thereafter it almost doubled every twenty years. Nothing like such a rate of growth had before been noted in the world, though it was closely paralleled in contemporary England. The settlement of great bodies of men in the West was eased by the removal of the Indian tribes from the regions east of the Mississippi. They had been defeated when they fought as allies of Britain in the war of 1812. Now it became Federal policy to eject them. The lands thus thrown open were made available in smaller units and at lower prices than in earlier years to the incoming colonists—for we might as well use this honourable word about them, unpopular though it may now be. Colonisation, in the true sense, was the task that engaged the Western pioneers. Farmers from stony New England were tilling the fertile empty territories to the south of the Great Lakes, while in the South the Black Belt of Alabama and Mississippi proved fruitful soil for the recent art of large-scale cotton cultivation.

But this ceaseless expansion to the West also changed the national centre of gravity, and intense stresses arose of interest as well as of feeling. The Eastern states, North and South alike, presently found their political power challenged by these settler communities, and the lure of pioneering created the fear of a labour shortage in the Eastern factories. In fact the gap was filled by new immigrants from Europe. As the frontier line rolled westward the new communities rising rapidly to statehood forced their own problems and desires upon the exhilarated but also embarrassed Federal Government. The East feared the approaching political dominance of the democratic West. The West resented the financial and economic bias of the Eastern moneyed classes. The forces of divergence grew strong, and only the elasticity of the Federal system around the core of state rights prevented the usual conflict between a mother country and its sturdy children.

The political history of these years between 1815 and 1830 is confused through the lack of adequate national party organisations to express the bitter sectional conflicts and hatreds in the North, South, and West. By 1830 the situation cleared and the great parties of the future stood opposed. With the growth of Federal legislation and the creation of a national economic framework of tariffs, banks, and land policies the Union felt the stress of state jealousies and rival interests. The expansion to the West tilted the political balance in favour of the new Western states, and strenuously the older forces in the North and South resisted the rising power of democracy within the Federal State. They had to confront not only the desires of the West, but also those of the small planters in the

South and of the working men in the industrial North. Many of these people now for the first time began to receive the vote as universal manhood suffrage was more widely adopted. The electorate was expanding and eager to make its voice heard. At the same time the convention system was introduced into American politics. Candidates for the Presidency and for lesser public office in the states gradually ceased to be nominated by restricted party caucuses. Instead they were selected at meetings of delegates representing a variety of local and specialised opinion. This obliged the would-be President and other public office-holders to be more responsive to the divergences of popular will. Politicians of conservative mind like Henry Clay and John C. Calhoun feared the menacing signs of particularism and the consequent threat to the Union. These men formulated what they called the "American System." But their policy was merely a re-expression of the ideas of Hamilton. They sought to harmonise economic interests within a Federal framework. As Calhoun had said in 1817, "We are greatly and rapidly—I was about to say fearfully—growing. This is our pride and our danger, our weakness and our strength. . . . Let us then bind the Republic together with a perfect system of roads and canals. Protection would make the parts adhere more closely. . . . It would form a new and most powerful cement."

Public works were set on foot; steamboats appeared upon the Mississippi, and the concentration of trade in the Gulf of Mexico roused alarm in the Atlantic states, who saw themselves being deprived of profitable markets. But they hastened themselves to compete with this increasing activity. In 1817 the state of New York began the construction of the Erie Canal, which was to make New York City the most prosperous of the Eastern seaports. The great Cumberland high-road across the Ohio to Illinois was built with Federal money, and a network of roads was to bind the eager West to the Eastern states. But the history of the American nineteenth century is dominated by the continually threatened cleavage of East and West, and, upon the Atlantic seaboard, of the Northern and Southern states. In the early years of the century the keynote of politics was the rival bidding of Northern and Southern politicians for the votes and support of the Western states.

*   *   *   *   *

The issue of slavery was soon to trouble the relations of the North and South. In 1819 a Bill was tabled in Congress to admit Missouri as a state to the Union. This territory lay inside the bounds of the Louisiana Purchase, where the future of slavery had not so far been decided by Federal law. As the people of Missouri proposed to allow slavery in their draft constitution the Northerners looked upon this Bill as an aggressive move to increase the voting power of the South. A wild campaign of mutual recrimination followed. But with the increasing problem of the West facing them both, North and South could not afford to quarrel, and the angry sectional strife stirred up by this Bill ended in a compromise which was to hold until the middle of the century. Missouri was admitted as a slave-holding state, and slavery was prohibited north of latitude 36° 30' within the existing territories of the Union which did not yet enjoy statehood. As part of the compromise Maine, which had just severed itself from Massachusetts, was admitted as a free state, making the division between slave and free equal, being twelve each. Far-seeing men realised the impending tragedy of this division. John Quincy Adams noted in his diary, "I considered it at once as the knell of the Union. I take it for granted that the present question is a mere preamble—a title-page to a great, tragic volume."

It was this cultured New Englander, son of the second President of the United States, who succeeded Monroe in 1825.

The so-called era of good feelings was coming to a close, and the four years of his Presidency were to reveal the growth of lively party politics. All the political and economic interests of the Eastern states were forced on to the defensive by the rapid expansion of the West.

The West grouped itself around the figure of the frontier General Andrew Jackson, who claimed to represent the true Jeffersonian principles of democracy against the corrupt moneyed interests of the East. Adams received the support of those classes who feared majority rule and viewed with alarm the growing power of the farmers and settlers of the frontier. The issue between the two factions was joined in 1828, when Jackson stood as rival candidate against Adams's re-election. In the welter of this election two new parties were born, the Democrats and the National Republicans, later called the Whigs. It was the fiercest campaign since Jefferson had driven the elder Adams from office in 1800. As the results came in it was seen that Adams had won practically nothing outside New England, and that in the person of Andrew Jackson the West had reached controlling power. Here at last was an American President who had no spiritual contacts whatever with the Old World or its projection on the Atlantic shore, who represented at the White House the spirit of the American frontier. To many it seemed that democracy had triumphed indeed.

There were wild scenes at Washington at the inauguration of the new President, dubbed by his opponent Adams as "the brawler from Tennessee." But to the men of the West Jackson was their General, marching against the political monopoly of the moneyed classes. The complications of high politics caused difficulties for the backwoodsman. His simple mind, suspicious of his opponents, made him open to influence by more partisan and self-seeking politicians. In part he was guided by Martin Van Buren, his Secretary of State. But he relied even more heavily for advice on political cronies of his own choosing, who were known as the "Kitchen Cabinet," because they were not office-holders. Jackson was led to believe that his first duty was to cleanse the stables of the previous régime. His dismissal of a large number of civil servants brought the spoils system, long prevalent in many states, firmly into the Federal machine.

Two great recurring problems in American politics, closely related, demanded the attention of President Andrew Jackson —the supremacy of the Union and the organisation of a national economy. Protection favoured the interests of the North at the expense of the South, and in 1832 the state of South Carolina determined to challenge the right of the Federal Government to impose a tariff system, and, echoing the Virginia and Kentucky resolutions of 1798, expounded in its most extreme form the doctrine of state rights. In the party struggles which followed the votes of the Western states held the balance. Their burning question was the regulation of the sale of public land by the Federal Government. As the historian S. E. Morison puts it, "It was all a game of balance between North, South, and West, each section offering to compromise a secondary interest in order to get votes for a primary interest. The South would permit the West to plunder the public domain, in return for a reduction of the tariff. The North offered the tempting bait of distribution [of the proceeds from land sales for public works in the West] in order to maintain protection. On the outcome of this sectional balance depended the alignment of parties in the future; even of the Civil War itself. Was it to be North and West against South, or South and West against North?" [1]

The debates on these themes in the American Senate con-

[1] *The Oxford History of the United States* (1927), vol. i, p. 391.

tained the finest examples of American oratory. In this battle of giants the most imposing of them all was Daniel Webster, of Massachusetts, the best speaker of his day. He it was who stated the case for the Union and refuted the case of South Carolina in one of the most famous of American speeches. His words enshrined the new feeling of nation-wide patriotism that was gathering strength, at least in the North. They show that New England in particular was moving away from the sectional views which had prevailed in 1812. A broader sense of loyalty to the Union was developing. "It is to that Union," Webster declared in the Senate, "we owe our safety at home, and our consideration and dignity abroad. It is to that Union that we are chiefly indebted for whatever makes us most proud of our country. That Union we reached only by the discipline of our virtues in the severe school of adversity. It had its origin in the necessities of disordered finance, prostrate commerce, and ruined credit. Under its benign influences these great interests immediately awoke, as from the dead, and sprang forth with newness of life. Every year of its duration has teemed with fresh proofs of its utility and its blessings; and although our territory has stretched out wider and wider, and our population spread farther and farther, they have not outrun its protection, or its benefits. It has been to us all a copious foundation of national, social and personal happiness.

"I have not allowed myself, Sir," he went on, "to look beyond the Union, to see what might lie hidden in the dark recess behind. I have not coolly weighed the chances of preserving liberty when the bonds that unite us together shall be broken asunder. I have not accustomed myself to hang over the precipice of disunion to see whether, with my short sight, I can fathom the depth of the abyss below; nor could I regard him as a safe counsellor in the affairs of this Government, whose thoughts should be mainly bent on considering, not how the Union may be best preserved, but how tolerable might be the condition of the people when it should be broken up and destroyed. While the Union lasts we have high, exciting, gratifying prospects spread out before us, for us and our children. Beyond that I seek not to penetrate the veil. God grant that in my day at least that curtain may not rise! God grant that on my vision never may be opened what lies behind! When my eyes shall be turned to behold for the last time the sun in heaven, may I not see him shining on the broken and dishonoured fragments of a once glorious Union; on states dissevered, discordant, belligerent; on a land rent with civil feuds, or drenched, it may be, in fraternal blood! Let their last feeble and lingering glance rather behold the gorgeous ensign of the Republic, now known and honoured throughout the earth, still full high advanced, its arms and trophies streaming in their original lustre, not a stripe erased or polluted, not a single star obscured, bearing for its motto no such miserable interrogatory as 'What is all this worth?' nor those other words of delusion and folly, 'Liberty first and Union afterwards,' but everywhere, spread all over in characters of living light, blazing on all its ample folds, as they float over the sea and over the land, and in every wind under the whole heavens, that other sentiment, dear to every true American heart—Liberty *and* Union, now and for ever, one and inseparable!"

On the Indiana frontier a young man was moved by this speech. His name was Abraham Lincoln.

President Jackson himself was impressed, and in his warlike approach to politics was prepared to coerce South Carolina by force. But a tactful compromise was reached. The tariff was lowered but rendered permanent, and the Force Act, authorising the President to use the Army if necessary to collect the customs duties, was declared null and void by

South Carolina. Here then for a space the matter was left. But the South Carolina theory of "nullification" showed the danger of the Republic, and with the prophetic instinct of the simple frontiersman Jackson pointed to the future: "The next pretext will be the negro or slavery question."

But the next serious issue was the Federal Bank, whose charter was due to come up for renewal in 1836. The National Republicans, or Whigs, now led by Clay, preferred to force it before the 1832 Presidential election. Jackson had long been expected to attack the moneyed power in politics. The position of the Bank illustrated the economic stresses which racked the American Republic. "It was an economic conflict," wrote Charles Beard, "that happened to take a sectional form: the people of the agricultural West had to pay tribute to Eastern capitalists on the money they had borrowed to buy land, make improvements, and engage in speculation." The contest was joined in the election. The triumphant return of Jackson to power was in fact a vote against the Bank of the United States. It was in vain that Daniel Webster was briefed as counsel for the Bank. Jackson informed the Bank president, "I do not dislike your bank more than all banks, but ever since I read the history of the South Sea Bubble I have been afraid of banks." He refused to consent to the passing of a Bill to renew the charter, and without waiting for the Bank to die a natural death in 1836 he decided at once to deprive it of Government deposits, which were sent to local banks throughout the states. When the charter expired it was not renewed, and for nearly thirty years there was no centralised banking system in the United States. The union of Western and Southern politicians had had their revenge upon the North. The Radicalism of the frontier had won a great political contest. Jackson's occupation of the Presidency had finally broken the "era of good feelings" which had followed the war with Britain, and by his economic policy he had split the old Republican Party of Jefferson. The Radicalism of the West was looked upon with widespread suspicion throughout the Eastern states, and Jackson's official appointments had not been very happy.

The election in 1836 of Jackson's lieutenant, Van Buren, meant the continuation of Jacksonian policy, while the old General himself returned in triumph to his retirement in Tennessee. The first incursions of the West into high politics had revealed the slumbering forces of democracy on the frontier and shown the inexperience of their leaders in such affairs.

*   *   *   *   *

The westward tide rolled on, bearing with it new problems of adjustment. The generation of the 1840's saw their culmination. During these years there took place the annexation of Texas, a war with Mexico, the conquest of California, and the settlement of the Oregon boundary with Great Britain. Adventurous Americans in search of land and riches had been since 1820 crossing the Mexican boundary into the Texas country, which belonged to the Republic of Mexico, freed from Spain in 1821. While this community was growing, American sailors on the Pacific coast, captains interested in the China trade, established themselves in the ports of the Mexican Province of California. Pioneers pushed their way overland in search of skins and furs, and by 1826 reached the mission stations of the Province. The Mexicans, alarmed at the appearance of these settlers, vainly sought to stem the flood; for Mexican Governments were highly unstable, and in distant Provinces their writ hardly ran. But there appeared on the scene a new military dictator, Santa Anna, determined to strengthen Mexican authority, and at once a revolt broke out. In November 1835 the Americans in Texas erected an autonomous state and raised the Lone Star flag. The Mexicans, under Santa Anna, marched northwards. At the Mission House of the Alamo in March 1836 a small body of Texans, fighting to the last man, was exterminated in one of the epic fights of American history by a superior Mexican force. The whole Province was aroused. Under the leadership of General Sam Houston from Tennessee a force was raised, and in savage fighting the Mexican army of Santa Anna was in its turn destroyed and its commander captured at San Jacinto River. The Texans had stormed the positions with the cry "Remember the Alamo!" The independence of Texas was recognised by Santa Anna. His act was repudiated later by the Mexican Government, but their war effort was exhausted, and the Texans organised themselves into a republic, electing Sam Houston as President.

For the next ten years the question of the admission of Texas as a state of the Union was a burning issue in American politics. As each new state demanded entry into the Union so the feeling for and against slavery ran higher. The great Abolitionist journalist, William Lloyd Garrison, called for a secession of the Northern states if the slave state of Texas was admitted to the Union. The Southerners, realising that Texan votes would give them a majority in the Senate if this vast territory was admitted as a number of separate states, clamoured for annexation. The capitalists of the East were committed, through the formation of land companies, to exploit Texas, and besides the issue of dubious stocks by these bodies vast quantities of paper notes and bonds of the new Texan Republic were floated in the United States. The speculation in these helped to split the political opposition of the Northern states to the annexation. Even more important was the conversion of many Northerners to belief in the "Manifest Destiny" of the United States. This meant that their destiny was to spread across the whole of the North American continent. The Democratic Party in the election of 1844 called for the occupation of Oregon as well as the annexation of Texas, thus holding out to the North the promise of Oregon as a counterweight to Southern Texas. The victory of the Democratic candidate, James K. Polk, was interpreted as a mandate for admitting Texas, and this was done by joint resolution of Congress in February 1845.

It remained to persuade Mexico to recognise this state of affairs, and also to fix the boundaries of Texas. President Polk was determined to push them as far south as possible, and war was inevitable. It broke out in May 1846. Meanwhile a similar train of events was unfolding on the other side of the continent. All this time American penetration of the West had continued, often with grim experiences of starvation and winter snows. Nothing could stop the migration towards the Pacific. The lure of the rich China trade and the dream of controlling the Western Ocean brought the acquisition of California to the fore, and gave her even more importance in American eyes than Texas. In June 1846 the American settlers in California, instigated from Washington, raised the Bear Flag as their standard of revolt and declared their independence on the Texan model. Soon afterwards American forces arrived and the Stars and Stripes replaced the Bear.

The American advance was rapidly gathering momentum. The Mexican army of the North was twice beaten by General Zachary Taylor, a future President. A force under General Winfield Scott was landed at Vera Cruz and marched on Mexico City. The capital fell to the Americans after a month of street fighting in September 1847. On this expedition a number of young officers distinguished themselves. They included Captain Robert E. Lee, Captain George B. McClellan,

Lieutenant Ulysses S. Grant, and Colonel Jefferson Davis.

Mexico sued for peace, and by the treaty which followed she was obliged not only to recognise the annexation of Texas, but also to cede California, Arizona, and New Mexico. Lieutenant Grant confided his impressions to his memoirs: "I do not think there was ever a more wicked war than that waged by the United States on Mexico. I thought so at the time, when I was a youngster, only I had not moral courage enough to resign." But the expansive force of the American peoples was explosive. "Manifest Destiny" was on the march, and it was unfortunate that Mexico stood in the path. The legend of Imperialism and the belief in the right of the United States to exploit both continents, North and South, which sprang from the Mexican War henceforward cast their shadow on co-operation between the South American republics and the United States.

*   *   *   *   *

The immediate gains were enormous. While the commissioners were actually debating the treaty with Mexico an American labourer in California discovered the first nugget of gold in that region. The whole economy of a sleepy Mexican province, with its age-old Spanish culture, was suddenly overwhelmed by a mad rush for gold. In 1850 the population of California was about eighty-two thousand souls. In two years the figure had risen to two hundred and seven thousand. A lawless mining society arose upon the Pacific coast. From the cities of the East and from the adjoining states men of all professions and classes of society flocked to California, many being murdered, killed in quarrels, by cold and famine, or drowned in the sea voyage round Cape Horn. The gold of California lured numbers to their death, and a few to riches beyond belief.

Oh! California,
That's the land for me;
I'm off to Sacramento
With my washbowl on my knee.

The anarchy of the gold rush brought an urgent demand
for settled government in California, and the old perplexing,
rasping quarrel over the admission of a new state was heard
again at Washington. For the moment nothing was done, and
the Californians called their own state convention and drew
up a temporary constitution.

During all this time, farther to the north, another territory
had been coming into being. The "Oregon Trail" had brought
many men from the more crowded states of the North-East
to find their homes and establish their farms along the un-
defined Canadian frontier to the Pacific. With the prospect
of war in the South for the acquisition of Texas and California, the American Government was not anxious to embark
upon a quarrel with Great Britain upon its Northern frontier.
There was strong opposition by the Southerners to the acquisition of Oregon, where the Northern pioneers were opposed to
slavery. Oregon would be another "free soil state." Negotiations were opened with Britain, and in spite of electioneering
slogans of "Fifty-four-forty or fight" the boundary was settled
in June 1846 by peaceful diplomacy along the forty-ninth
parallel. This solution owed much to the accommodating nature of the Foreign Secretary in Peel's Government, Lord Ab-
erdeen. The controversy now died down, and in 1859 the territory of Oregon reached statehood.

Among the many settlements which lay dotted over the
whole of the American continent the strangest perhaps was
the Mormon colony at Salt Lake City. In the spring of 1847

members of this revivalist and polygamist sect started from the state of Illinois under their prophet leader, Brigham Young, to find homes free from molestation in the West. By the summer they reached the country round Salt Lake, and two hours after their arrival they had begun establishing their homes and ploughing up the soil. Within three years a flourishing community of eleven thousand souls, combining religious fervour, philoprogenitiveness, and shrewd economic sense, had been established by careful planning in the Salt Lake country, and in 1850 the territory received recognition by the Federal Government under the name of Utah. The colony was established in a key position on the trail which led both to Oregon and California. The sale of food and goods to the travellers and adventurers who moved in both directions along this route brought riches to the Mormon settler, and Salt Lake City, soon tainted, it is true, by the introduction of more lawless and unbelieving elements, became one of the richest cities in America.

With the establishment of this peculiar colony the settlement of the continent was comprehensive. The task before the Federal Government was now to organise the Far Western territory won in the Mexican War and in the compromise with Britain. From this there rose in its final and dread form the issue of bond and free.

ABRAHAM LINCOLN

Sixteenth President of the United States

JEFFERSON DAVIS
President of the Confederate States

Fort Sumter 1861

FORT SUMTER
In Confederate hands after the two day's bombardment in April 1861

LINCOLN'S CALL TO ARMS

The 67th New York Infantry at Camp Proctor in the summer of 1861

CHAPTER TWO

Slavery and Secession

IN the years following 1850 the prospects of the United States filled America with hope and Europe with envious admiration. The continent had been conquered and nourished. Exports, imports, and, most of all, internal trade, had been more than doubled in a decade. The American mercantile marine outnumbered the ships under the British flag. Nearly £50,000,000 in gold was added to the coinage in the years 1851 and 1852. More than thirty thousand miles of railway overcame the vast distances, and added economic cohesion to political unity. Here democracy, shielded by the oceans and the Royal Navy from European dangers, founded upon English institutions and the Common Law, stimulated by the impulse of the French Revolution, seemed at last to have achieved both prosperity and power. The abounding industrialism of the Eastern states was balanced and fed by an immense agriculture of yeomen farmers. In all material affairs the American people surpassed anything that history had known before.

Yet thoughtful men and travellers had for some years observed the approach of a convulsion which would grip not only the body but the soul of the United States. Of the three races who dwelt in North America, the Whites towered overwhelming and supreme. The Red Men, the original inhabitants, age-long product of the soil and climate, shrank back, pushed, exploited, but always disdainful, from the arms, and still more from the civilisation, of the transplanted European society by which they were ousted and eclipsed. The Black Men presented a problem, moral, social, economic, and political, the like of which had never before been known. It was said that both these races were downtrodden by White ascendancy as truly as animals are mastered, used, or exterminated by mankind. The proud Redskin was set upon his road to ruin by an excessive liberty. Almost all the four million Negroes were slaves.

In regions so wide and varied as those of the Union extreme divergences of interest, outlook, and culture had developed. South of the fortieth parallel and the projecting angle formed by the Mississippi and the Ohio the institution of Negro slavery had long reigned almost unquestioned. Upon this basis the whole life of the Southern states had been erected. It was a strange, fierce, old-fashioned life. An aristocracy of planters, living in rural magnificence and almost feudal state, and a multitude of smallholders, grew cotton for the world by slave-labour. Of the six million white inhabitants of the so-called "slave states" less than three hundred and fifty thousand owned slaves, and only forty thousand controlled plantations requiring a working unit of more than twenty field hands. But the three or four thousand principal slave-owners generally ruled the politics of the South as effectively as the medieval baronage had ruled England. Beneath them, but not dissociated from them, were, first, several hundred thousand small slave-owners, to whom "the peculiar institution," as it had already come to be called, was a domestic convenience; second, a strong class of yeomen farmers similar to that existing in the North; and, thirdly, a rabble of "mean whites" capable of being formed into an army.

There was a grace and ease about the life of the white men in the South that was lacking in the bustling North. It was certainly not their fault that these unnatural conditions had arisen. For two centuries the slave trade in African Negroes with the New World had been a staple enterprise in Spain, in

France, and above all in England. Vast numbers of black men, caught upon the west coast of Africa, had been transported like cattle across the Atlantic to be the property of their purchasers. They had toiled and multiplied. The bulk had become adapted to their state of life, which, though odious to Christian civilisation, was physically less harsh than African barbarism. The average Negro slave, like the medieval serf, was protected by his market value, actual and procreative, as well as by the rising standards of society, from the more senseless and brutal forms of ill-usage.

The planters of the South, and the slaves they owned, had both grown up in wide, unkempt lands without ever having known any other relationship. Now, suddenly, in the midst of the nineteenth century, dire challenge was hurled at the whole system and the society in which it was engrained. A considerable, strongly characterised, and slowly matured community found itself subjected to the baleful and scandalised glare of the Christian world, itself in vigorous and self-confident progress. They had long dwelt comfortably upon the fertile slopes of a volcano. Now began the rumblings, tremors, and exhalations which portended a frightful eruption.

It is almost impossible for us nowadays to understand how profoundly and inextricably Negro slavery was interwoven into the whole life, economy, and culture of the Southern states. The tentacles of slavery spread widely through the Northern "free" states, along every channel of business dealing and many paths of political influence. One assertion alone reveals the powerlessness of the community to shake itself free from the frightful disease which had become part of its being. It was said that over six hundred and sixty thousand slaves were held by ministers of the Gospel and members of the different Protestant Churches. Five thousand Methodist ministers owned two hundred and nineteen thousand slaves;

six thousand five hundred Baptists owned a hundred and twenty-five thousand; one thousand four hundred Episcopalians held eighty-eight thousand; and so on. Thus the institution of slavery was not only defended by every argument of self-interest, but many a Southern pulpit championed it as a system ordained by the Creator and sanctified by the Gospel of Christ.

It had not always been so. During the Revolution against King George III many Southerners had expressed the hope that slavery would eventually be abolished. But as time passed "the peculiar institution" became, in the words of Morison and Commager, "so necessary that it ceased to appear evil." [1] By the 1830's Southerners were ready to defend slavery as a positive good and a permanent basis for society. This was a striking change of opinion for which there were several reasons. The rapid growth of cotton cultivation called for a large labour force which according to Southerners could only be provided by Negroes in a state of slavery. Moreover, widespread fears had been aroused in the South by a number of slave insurrections in which some whites had been massacred. If the Negro were freed, it was asked, would a white man's life be safe? or, to press the question more closely home, a white woman's honour? In earlier times hopeful philanthropists had thought to solve the problem by shipping the Negroes back to Africa and setting them up in their own republic. The state of Liberia had thus come into existence. But attempts to carry this plan further were abandoned. It was too expensive. Besides, the Negroes preferred America. For Southerners there was an alarming example near at hand of what happened when slaves were freed. In the British West Indies, as elsewhere in the British Empire, slavery had been abolished by the Act passed in 1833. This was one of the

[1] *The Growth of the American Republic*, vol. i, p. 246.

great reforms achieved by the Whig Government of Earl Grey. The planters of the West Indies, who led a life much like that of Southern gentlemen, were paid compensation for the loss of their human property. Nevertheless their fortunes promptly and visibly declined. All this could be perceived by men of reflection on the neighbouring American mainland.

Meanwhile the North, once largely indifferent to the fate of slaves, had been converted by the 1850's to the cause of anti-slavery. For twenty years William Lloyd Garrison's newspaper, *The Liberator,* had been carrying on from Boston a campaign of the utmost virulence against the institution of slavery. This public print was not very widely read, but its language enraged the South. At the same time the American Anti-Slavery Society in New York and other humanitarian bodies were issuing vigorous tracts and periodicals. They employed scores of agents to preach Abolition up and down the land. The result was a hardening of sentiment on both sides of the question. It was hardened still further in 1852, when Harriet Beecher Stowe published *Uncle Tom's Cabin.* Her work was frankly propagandist; she used every weapon. In its pages the theoretical and religious arguments are bandied to and fro, but there was one method in which she excelled all other assailants of the evil. She presented to her readers a succession of simple, poignant incidents inseparable from a system of slavery: the breaking up of the Negro's home and family, the parting of husband and wife, the sale of the baby from the breast of its mother; the indiscriminate auction of the slaves on the death of a good employer; the impotence of the virtuous slave-owner, the cruelties of the bad; the callous traffic of the slave-dealers, and the horrors of the remote plantations, the whipping establishments to which fine ladies sent their maids for chastisement for minor faults; the aggravated problem of the quadroon and the mulatto; the almost-white slave girl sold and resold for lust; the bringing into the world of slave children indistinguishable in their colour from the dominant race—all these features of the life of a civilised, educated, modern Christian community, occupying enormous fertile regions of the earth, were introduced with every trapping of art and appeal into her pages.

Such advocacy was devastating. By the end of the year hundreds of thousands of copies of *Uncle Tom's Cabin* had been sold in the United States. In September, it is said, ten thousand copies of it were being supplied every day to a single firm of English booksellers. By the end of 1852 more than a million copies had been sold in England, probably ten times as many as had ever been sold of any other work except the Bible and the Prayer Book. *Uncle Tom's Cabin* rolled round the world in every language and was read with passion and emotion in every country. It was the herald of the storm.

* * * * *

The moral surge of the age had first suppressed, by naval power, the slave trade on the seas, and thereafter—the young Mr Gladstone notwithstanding—abolished the status of slavery throughout the British Empire. The same temper stirred alike the New England states of the Atlantic shore and the powerful, swiftly growing population of the Middle West of the American Union. A gulf of sentiment and interest opened and widened between the Northern and Southern states. Across this gulf there flashed for some years the interchanges of thought, of argument and parley. In the North many of the leaders, religious and secular, felt intensely that the whole future of the noble continent they had won lay under a curse. If it could not at once be lifted, at least it must be prevented from spreading. Nor was this passion in any degree excited, in its earliest phase, by commercial rivalry. There was no doubt that slave labour could not hold its own with free labour in tilling the soil where the climatic conditions were similar. The contrast between the activity and progress of a free state on the Ohio and the stagnation of a slave state on the opposite bank was glaringly apparent to all beholders. It was the contrast between the nineteenth century and the seventeenth. The Northern states were not undersold by the competition of the South. They also needed the cotton crop in which alone slave labour was an economic advantage. The issue was not economic, but moral. It was also social. The slave-owning aristocracy in much of the South felt a class-superiority to the business, manufacturing, and financial society of the North. The Puritan stock of the North regarded the elegant gentry of the South with something of the wrath and censure of Cromwell's Ironsides for Rupert's Cavaliers. Indeed, at many points the grim struggle which impended resembled and reproduced in its passions the antagonisms of the English Civil War.

But the actual occasion of quarrel was political and constitutional. The North held tenaciously to the Federal conceptions of Alexander Hamilton. In the South Jefferson's idea of sovereign state rights was paramount. Many of the Southern Generals, like Joseph E. Johnston, Ambrose P. Hill, and FitzHugh Lee, had never owned a slave. A Virginian colonel of the United States Army serving in Texas, Robert E. Lee, wrote that slavery was "a moral and political evil in any country," as few in an enlightened age could but acknowledge. But upon the constitutional issue all these men of the highest morale and virtue deemed themselves bound to the death to the fortunes and sovereign independence of their states. The North, it was said, was enriching itself at the expense of the South. The Yankees were jealous of a style and distinction to which vulgar commercialism could never attain. They had no right to use the Federal Constitution which the great Virginians Washington and Madison had largely founded, in order to bind the most famous states of the Union to their dictates. They did not understand the totally different conditions of Southern life. They maligned and insulted a civilisation more elevated in manners, if not in worldly wealth, than their own. They sought to impose the tyranny of their ideas upon states which had freely joined the Union for common purposes, and might as freely depart when those purposes had been fulfilled.

The old Missouri compromise of 1820, namely, that latitude 36° 30′ should divide freedom from slavery in the territories of the Louisiana Purchase, no longer satisfied the passions now aroused. By the Mexican War extensive new territories had been acquired; what principle should be applied to them? The Southerners, still dominated by that great figure of the 1812 generation, John C. Calhoun, held that the territories belonged to the states united, not to the United States, that slaves were Common Law property, and that Congress had no right to prohibit slavery in the Territories. The demand of California for admission to the Union precipitated the crisis. Many moderates had wanted to prolong the line of the Missouri compromise across the continent to the Pacific. But in California it did not meet the case. It would have run right through the middle of the state. Besides, the constitution of California prohibited slavery, and its introduction would set a precedent in those states which were to be created out of the conquests from Mexico. In January 1850 the gathering storm-clouds of slavery and secession evoked in the Senate the last of the great oratorical debates in which Calhoun, Clay, and Webster vied with one another. Henry Clay produced his last compromise in resolutions to postpone collision. California should be admitted to the Union immediately as a "free" state;

the territorial Governments in New Mexico and Utah should be organised without mentioning slavery; a stringent Fugitive Slave Law would appease the South, and the assumption of the Texas National Debt by the Federal Government the bond-holders of the North. By these mutual concessions Clay hoped to preserve the political unity of the continent. On this last occasion he rose and spoke for nearly two days in the Senate. Calhoun was dying, and sat grimly silent in the Senate. One of his colleagues spoke his plea for him. "I have, Senators, believed from the first that the agitation of the subject of slavery would, if not prevented by some timely and effective measure, end in disunion. . . . The cords that bind the states together are snapping." Beneath the slavery problem lay the root fear of the Southern states that economically and politically they were being oppressed by the North and losing in the race for allies in the Western states.

Daniel Webster rose three days later: "I speak to-day for the preservation of the Union. Hear me for my cause." The voices of Webster and Clay prevailed and the compromise was adopted. Passions were for the moment stilled by what was called the "principle of popular sovereignty." This meant that when the new Territories became states the settlers should decide for themselves for or against slavery. Calhoun was already dead, and within two years Clay and Webster passed from the scene. They left behind them an uneasy calm. Meanwhile the continent developed at dizzy speed. By 1850 nine thousand miles of railway had been built; by 1861 over thirty thousand. German and Irish immigrants from Europe streamed into the new lands of the West. Agricultural machinery changed the settler type. The prairie farmer replaced the backwoodsman, and the cultivation of the Great Plains began in earnest.

*   *   *   *   *

A fresh cause of divergence sprang from the choice of the transcontinental railway route. The rival interests of North and South were decisively involved, and in the political dispute the North and West drew together. The southern route was the shortest to the Pacific coast, and passed through organised territories from New Orleans to Texas and thence by the Gila valley to San Diego. The northern followed the natural trail of emigration which bound California and Oregon to the states bordering the Great Lakes. In between lay a third route through regions as yet unorganised, but in which Northern capital was invested. Senator Stephen A. Douglas of Illinois, who ardently wished to promote the settlement of the West and was heavily committed to the central line, became the champion of Northern interests. In order to organise this central zone he proposed in January 1854 a Bill establishing the territory of Nebraska. As a bait for Southern votes he included a clause embodying the conception of "popular sovereignty." This changed the issue and aggravated the dispute. People in the North had taken the compromise of 1850 to apply only to the former Mexican territories. Now it was proposed to introduce it into regions where hitherto the line of the Missouri compromise had prevailed. As these areas of the Great Plains were north of latitude 36° 30′ the new Bill implicitly repealed the Missouri Compromise Act. The Southerners wished this to be done explicitly, and Douglas agreed. This might carry slavery north of the line.

The anti-slavery forces in the North, already furious with Douglas, were determined to resist the introduction of slavery into the new territories. In May the Kansas-Nebraska Act was passed by the Senate. The new territories of the Great Plains were to be divided into Kansas and Nebraska, and the principle of "popular sovereignty" was affirmed. This Act was a signal for outbursts of agitation and violence in the Northern states. Under the Fugitive Slave Law Federal agents had already been instructed to arrest and send back to their masters slaves who had escaped into the free states. There had been innumerable minor incidents, but now, on the morrow of the Kansas-Nebraska Act, the patience of the North was at an end. The day after it came into force a Boston mob attempted to rescue a fugitive slave, Anthony Burns, who was detained for deportation to the South. It took a battalion of artillery, four platoons of marines, the sheriff's posse, and twenty-two companies of the militia to line the streets and bring the slave to the ship at Boston wharf. "It cost the United States about a hundred thousand dollars to return the slave to his master. The real bill came later, and it was paid in blood." [1]

In the new territory of Kansas there was murderous faction fighting between the free-soil and pro-slavery partisans. Slavery-men sacked the free-soil town of Lawrence, and three days later John Brown, a Puritanical mystic and militant Abolitionist from Ohio, with his four sons, dragged five slavery-men from their beds and slaughtered them as a reprisal. Over two hundred lives were lost in this local reign of terror, but John Brown escaped. At every point, in every walk of life, the opposing causes came into conflict. A Senator from Massachusetts was beaten over the head with a cane in the Senate by a South Carolina Representative till he was unconscious. All the anti-slavery elements in the North and West had coalesced after the passing of the Kansas-Nebraska Act in a new Republican Party upon the platform of anti-slavery. Feeling ran high in the Presidential elections of 1856. But Democratic influences nominated "a Northern man with Southern principles," James Buchanan of Pennsylvania, and

[1] Morison and Commager, *Growth of the American Republic,* vol. i, p. 622.

for the last time Southern influences had their voice at Washington.

Two days after the inauguration of the new President the Supreme Court published its decision upon the famous case of the slave Dred Scott versus his master, Sanford. Scott had been taken by his master from slave-owning Missouri to the free state of Illinois and then to Wisconsin Territory. He sued for his freedom on the grounds that residence in those two places had made him a free man. The questions before the Court were two. Was Scott a citizen of Missouri, which he needed to be to have the right to bring an action? And had his residence elsewhere changed his established status? The Court decided against him on both points. Chief Justice Taney delivered a judgment which, while it expressed the law as it existed under the Costitution, provoked a storm throughout the North. "The negro," declared Taney, "was not a citizen in the eyes of the Constitution, which was 'made for white men only.'" He could not sue in any court of the United States. The Negroes were regarded as "so far inferior that they had no rights which the white man was bound to respect." The slave was the property of his owner, and the National Government was nowhere given power over the property of the inhabitants of the United States. It had no right to prohibit slavery in the Territories, and the old Missouri compromise, on which Scott had in part relied for his freedom, was constitutionally wrong. Thus the Supreme Court. It is fair to add that Taney remarked it was not within the province of the Court to decide whether the Founding Fathers had been right to regard the Negro in this way. And in fact Dred Scott was immediately freed after the verdict. His had been a case purposefully designed to test the law and inflame opinion. This it certainly did. The Republican Party, which had been launched to prevent slavery spreading into the Territories, saw its whole programme declared unconstitutional. "The people of the United States," cried William H. Seward, a Republican leader, "never can and never will accept principles so abhorrent."

The savage struggle between free-soil and slavery in the Great Plains brought from the backwoods into national politics a new figure. Abraham Lincoln, a small-town lawyer from Springfield, Illinois, was stirred to the depths of his being by the passing of the Kansas-Nebraska Act. He had already served a term in Congress; now he stood for the Senate. He espoused the duty of opposing by the moral force of his personality the principle of slavery. " 'A house divided against itself cannot stand.' I believe this Government cannot endure permanently half slave and half free. I do not expect the Union to be dissolved—I do not expect the house to fall—but I do expect it will cease to be divided. It will become all one thing or all the other. Either the opponents of slavery will arrest the further spread of it, and place it where the public mind shall rest in the belief that it is in the course of ultimate extinction; or its advocates will push it forward till it shall become alike lawful in all the states, old as well as new, North as well as South." In a series of public debates and speeches Lincoln fought Douglas throughout the prairie towns of Illinois in the summer and autumn of 1858, and although he was beaten for the Senatorship he had already become a national figure. He had made slavery a moral and not a legal issue, and he had propounded the disruptive idea of overriding the Supreme Court decision and of outlawing slavery in the new territories. He felt instinctively the weakness and impermanence of this new concession to the susceptibilities of the South. He realised that as the agitation for abolition grew, so the Southerners would demand further guarantees to protect their own peculiar slave society. President Buchanan and the

Democratic circle around the White House talked of conquering Cuba and Nicaragua in the hope of adding new slave-owning territories to the Union. Southern business men urged reopening the slave trade owing to the high price of slaves, while all the time the North, in a series of disturbing incidents, defied the Fugitive Slave Act of 1850.

It needed but a spark to cause an explosion. In October 1859 the fanatic John Brown, with his sons and a dozen followers, seized the Federal arsenal at Harpers Ferry, on the slavery frontier, declared war upon the United States, and liberated a number of bewildered slaves. He was attacked by the Federal marines under Colonel Robert E. Lee, and after some loss of life was captured, severely wounded. He was tried and hanged with four of his adherents. The South, declaring the outrage the work of the Republican Party, was convulsed with excitement. In the North millions regarded John Brown as a martyr. His body lay mouldering in the grave, but his soul went marching on.

CHAPTER THREE

The Union in Danger

NOW came the fateful Presidential election of 1860. In February the Southern Senator Jefferson Davis demanded that the Northern states should repeal their Personal Liberty Laws and cease to interfere with the Fugitive Slave Law of 1850. Chief Justice Taney's decision of the Supreme Court must be obeyed. Slavery could not be prohibited by the Federal Government in the Territories of the United States. Rather, Davis demanded, the Federal Government should protect slavery in those areas. Against this, Abraham Lincoln, in New York and elsewhere, unfolded in magnificent orations, calm, massive, and magnanimous, the anti-slavery cause. In this crisis the Democratic Party split. When Douglas, their Presidential candidate, carried a set of compromise proposals in the party meeting at Charleston the Alabama delegation marched out of the hall, followed by those of seven other cotton states. Lincoln would probably in any case have been elected, but the division among the Democrats made his victory certain. The cotton states put forward as their candidate John C. Breckinridge, of Kentucky, who was at that moment Vice-President. He stood as a Southern Rights Democrat. The scene was further complicated by the appearance of a fourth aspirant, Senator John Bell, of Kentucky, who called himself a Constitutional Unionist and was an old-fashioned Whig. Secession was not the issue, though everyone felt that the South would in fact secede if Lincoln won. Slavery was the dominating and all-absorbing topic. Lincoln and the Republicans wanted to reverse the Dred Scott decision, prohibit slavery in the Territories and confine it within its existing limits. Douglas and the official Democrats were for non-intervention in the Territories and "popular sovereignty" by the settlers. Breckinridge and his supporters demanded that slavery in the Territories should be protected by law. Bell tried to ignore the issue altogether in the blissful hope that the nation could be made to forget everything that had happened since the Mexican War. On November 6, 1860, Lincoln was elected. He had behind him only 40 per cent of the voters. Douglas was the runner-up on the popular vote. Breckinridge, who was reputed to be the Secessionist candidate in spite of his assurances of loyalty to the Union, came third. Even in the slave states he failed to win a majority of the votes.

In spite of this great majority against breaking the Union, the state of South Carolina, where the doctrines of Calhoun were cherished, passed by a unanimous vote at Charleston on December 20 its famous Ordinance of Secession, declaring that the Union of 1788 between South Carolina and all other states, Northern and Southern alike, was dissolved. This precipitate and mortal act was hailed with delirious enthusiasm. The cannons fired; the bells rang; flags flew on every house. The streets were crowded with cheering multitudes. The example of South Carolina was followed by the states of Mississippi, Florida, Alabama, Georgia, Louisiana, and Texas. Delegates from the first of these sovereign states, as they regarded themselves, met in Alabama in February and organised a new Confederacy, of which Jefferson Davis was chosen President. A new constitution, similar in almost all respects to that of the United States, but founded explicitly upon slav-

**GENERAL
ROBERT E. LEE**

Commander-in-Chief of
the Confederate Army

**GENERAL THOMAS
("STONEWALL")
JACKSON**

Lee's "great lieutenant"

THE *MONITOR*

"The *Merrimac* had made the naval revolution, but the *Monitor,* one day later, was a whole lap ahead of her."

CIVIL WAR

Friends and even relatives met on opposite sides during the conflict. Here, on the left, sits Lieutenant J. B. Washington, captured by Federal troops on the morning of May 31, 1862, after the battle of Seven Pines. Later that day a classmate from West Point joined him for this photograph to be taken. His name was Lieutenant George A. Custer, of the Fifth U. S. Cavalry, who was later to achieve fame as a cavalry general and Indian fighter.

AFTER THE BATTLE OF GAINES'S MILL

On June 30, 1862, Confederate troops under General Magruder captured Savage's Station. Among their prisoners were some 2,500 wounded Federal soldiers brought there after the battle of Gaines's Mill on the 27th.

THE BRIDGE AT HARPERS FERRY

Captured by Jackson on September 15, 1862

THE BATTLE OF THE ANTIETAM

The post and rail fence on the Hagerstown pike, where on September 17, 1862, the Confederate left, under Jackson, attempted to rally in the face of Hooker's charge

"Bloody Lane," the sunken road connecting the Hagerstown and Keedysville turnpikes, where on September 17 the Confederate troops under General D. H. Hill held out for four hours against the Federal divisions of Generals French and Richardson

AFTER THE BATTLE OF THE ANTIETAM

Dr. A. Hurd, of the Fourteenth Indiana Volunteers, at a "field hospital," established after the battle

PRESIDENT LINCOLN AND GENERAL McCLELLAN

The meeting of October 4, 1862, on the battlefield of Antietam.
"He told me that he was satisfied with all that I had done, that he
would stand by me," said the General-in-Chief of the Federal Army

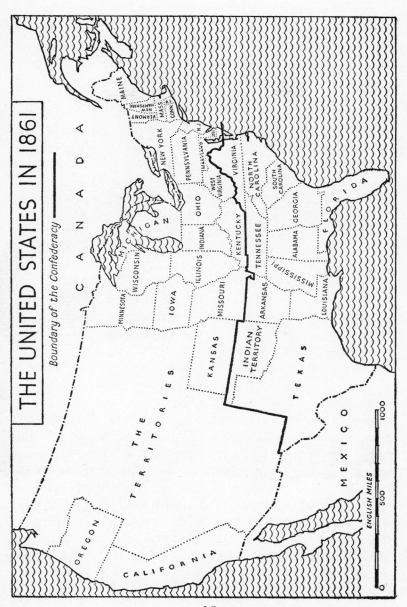

THE UNITED STATES IN 1861

Boundary of the Confederacy ———

CANADA

MAINE
VERMONT
NEW HAMPSHIRE
MASS.
CONN.
R.I.
NEW YORK
PENNSYLVANIA
NEW JERSEY
DEL.
MARYLAND
VIRGINIA
WEST VIRGINIA
NORTH CAROLINA
SOUTH CAROLINA
OHIO
MICHIGAN
INDIANA
KENTUCKY
TENNESSEE
GEORGIA
ALABAMA
MISSISSIPPI
FLORIDA
ILLINOIS
WISCONSIN
MINNESOTA
IOWA
MISSOURI
ARKANSAS
LOUISIANA
KANSAS
INDIAN TERRITORY
TEXAS
THE TERRITORIES
OREGON
CALIFORNIA
MEXICO

ENGLISH MILES
1000
500
0

ery, was proclaimed. A Confederate flag—the Stars and Bars—was adopted. President Davis was authorised to raise an army of a hundred thousand men, large sums were voted, ·and a delegation of three was sent abroad to seek recognition and friendship in Europe. All the leading figures concerned in this decision harboured grave illusions. They thought the North would not try to coerce them back into the Union. If it made the attempt they believed the Yankees would be no match for Southern arms. And if the North imposed a blockade the Confederates expected that the Powers of Europe would intervene on their behalf. They cherished the notion that "King Cotton" was so vital to Britain and France that neither country could peaceably allow its supplies to be cut off.

Buchanan was still President of the United States, and Lincoln, President-Elect, could not take office till March. For four months the dying administration gaped upon a distracted land. Floyd, Secretary of War, an ardent Southerner, showed no particular vigilance or foresight. He tamely allowed muskets which had been sent North for alterations to be returned to the Southern arsenals. Every facility was given to officers of the Regular Army to join the new forces being feverishly raised in the South. Buchanan, longing for release, tried desperately to discharge his duties and follow a middle course. All counter-preparations in the North were paralysed. On the other hand, he refused to recognise the validity of secession. Practically all the Federal posts, with their small garrisons, in the Southern states had passed without fighting into the possession of the Confederacy. But the forts of Charleston harbour, under the command of Major Anderson, a determined officer, continued to fly the Stars and Stripes. When called upon to surrender he withdrew to Fort Sumter,

which stood on an island. His food ran low, and when a ship
bearing supplies from the North arrived to succour him Confederate batteries from the mainland drove it back by can-
non-fire. Meanwhile strenuous efforts at compromise were
being made. Many Northerners were prepared for the sake of
peace to give way to the South on the slavery issue. But Lincoln was inflexible. He would not repudiate the platform on
which he had been elected. He could not countenance the extension of slavery to the Territories. This was the nub on
which all turned. In this tense and tremendous situation
Abraham Lincoln was sworn President on March 4, 1861.
Around him the structure of Federal Government was falling
to pieces. Officials and officers were every day leaving for
their home states in the South. Hands were clasped between
old comrades for the last time in friendship.

The North, for all its detestation of slavery, had by no
means contemplated civil war. Between the extremists on
both sides there was an immense borderland where all interests and relationships were interlaced by every tie of kinship
and custom and every shade of opinion found its expression.
So far only the cotton states, or Lower South, had severed
themselves from the Union. Missouri, Arkansas, Kentucky,
Tennessee, North Carolina, Maryland, Delaware, and above
all the noble and ancient Virginia, the Old Dominion, the
birthplace of Washington, the fountain of American tradition
and inspiration, still hung in the balance. Lincoln appealed
for patience and conciliation. He declared himself resolved to
hold the forts and property of the United States. He dis-
claimed all intention of invading the South. He announced
that he would not interfere with slavery in the Southern
states. He revived the common memories of the North and
South, which, like "mystic cords, stretch from every battle-

field and patriot grave to every living heart . . . over this broad land." "In your hands," he exclaimed, "my dissatisfied fellow-countrymen, and not in mine, is this momentous issue of civil war. The Government will not assail you. You can have no conflict without yourselves being the aggressors. You have no oath registered in Heaven to destroy the Government, while I shall have the most solemn one to preserve and defend it."

On April 8 Lincoln informed the Governor of South Carolina of his intention to re-victual Major Anderson and his eighty-three men in Fort Sumter. Thereupon President Davis ordered General Beauregard, who commanded seven thousand men at Charleston, to demand the immediate surrender of the fort. Anderson, admitting that famine would reduce him in a few days, nevertheless continued constant. Vain parleys were held; but before dawn on April 12 the Confederate batteries opened a general bombardment, and for two days fifty heavy cannon rained their shells upon Fort Sumter. Anderson and his handful of men, sheltering in their bomb-proof caverns, feeling that all had been done that honour and law required, marched out begrimed and half suffocated on the 14th, and were allowed to depart to the North. No blood had been shed, but the awful act of rebellion had occurred.

The cannonade at Fort Sumter resounded through the world. It roused and united the people of the North. All the free states stood together. Party divisions were effaced. Douglas, Lincoln's rival at the election, with a million and a half Democratic votes at his back, hastened to the White House to grasp Lincoln's hand. Ex-President Buchanan declared, "The North will sustain the administration almost to a man." Upon this surge and his own vehement resolve, Lincoln issued a proclamation calling for "the militia of the Union to the number of seventy-five thousand" to suppress "combinations" in seven states "too powerful to be suppressed by the ordinary course of judicial proceedings." Here, then, was the outbreak of the American Civil War.

* * * * *

Upon Lincoln's call to arms to coerce the seceding states Virginia made without hesitation the choice which she was so heroically to sustain. She would not fight on the issue of slavery, but stood firm on the constitutional ground that every state in the Union enjoyed sovereign rights. On this principle Virginians denied the claim of the Federal Government to exercise coercion. By eighty-eight votes to fifty-five the Virginia Convention at Richmond refused to allow the state militia to respond to Lincoln's call. Virginia seceded from the Union and placed her entire military forces at the disposal of the Confederacy. This decided the conduct of one of the noblest Americans who ever lived, and one of the greatest captains known to the annals of war.

Robert E. Lee stood high in American life. His father had been a colonel in the Revolution. By his marriage with Miss Custis, a descendant of Mrs George Washington, he became the master of Arlington, the house overlooking the national capital which George Custis, Washington's adopted son, "the child of Mount Vernon," as he was called, had built for himself a few miles from Washington's own home. A graduate of West Point, General Scott's Engineer Staff-Officer in the Mexican War, Lee had served for more than twenty-five years in the United States Army with distinction. His noble presence and gentle, kindly manner were sustained by religious faith and an exalted character. As the American scene darkened he weighed carefully, while commanding a regiment of cavalry on the Texan border, the course which duty and honour would require from him. He was opposed to slavery and thought that "secession would do no good," but he had been taught from childhood that his first allegiance was to the state of Virginia. Summoned to Washington during March 1861, he had thus expressed himself to an intimate Northern friend: "If Virginia stands by the old Union, so will I. But if she secedes (though I do not believe in secession as a constitutional right, nor that there is sufficient cause for revolution), then I will still follow my native state with my sword, and if need be with my life."

He reached the capital in the fevered days of March, and General Scott, his old chief, wrestled earnestly with him in a three hours' interview. By Lincoln's authority he was offered the chief command of the great Union army now being raised. He declined at once, and when a day later Virginia seceded he resigned his commission, bade farewell for ever to his home at Arlington, and in the deepest sorrow boarded the train for Richmond. Here he was immediately offered the chief command of all the military and naval forces of Virginia. He had resigned his United States commission on the Saturday, and on the Monday following he accepted his new task. Some of those who saw him in these tragic weeks, when sometimes his eyes filled with tears, emotion which he never showed after the gain or loss of great battles, have written about his inward struggle. But there was no struggle; he never hesitated. The choice was for the state of Virginia. He deplored that choice; he foresaw its consequences with bitter grief; but for himself he had no doubts at the time, nor ever after regret or remorse.

Those who hold that the fortunes of mankind are largely the result of the impact upon events of superior beings will find it fitting that Lee's famous comrade in arms, "Stonewall Jackson," should be mentioned at this point. Lee was fifty-four in the crisis, Jackson but thirty-seven. Like Lee, he was a trained professional soldier who had served gallantly in the

Mexican War. He had devoted himself to the theoretical study of the military art. He was at this time a professor at the Virginia Military Institute. Jackson came of Ulster stock, settled in Virginia. His character was stern, his manner reserved and usually forbidding, his temper Calvinistic, his mode of life strict, frugal, austere. He might have stepped into American history from the command of one of Cromwell's regiments. There burned in him a hatred of Northern domination not to be found in Lee. Black-bearded, pale-faced, with thin, compressed lips, aquiline nose, and dark, piercing eyes, he slouched in his weather-stained uniform a professor-warrior; yet greatly beloved by the few who knew him best, and gifted with that strange power of commanding measureless devotion from the thousands whom he ruled with an iron hand.

Both these men, though they habitually spoke and no doubt convinced themselves to the contrary, loved war as a technical art to which their lives had been given. Their sayings and letters abound with expressions of sorrow at the terrible decrees of which they had now become the servants. But on a long night march to a desprate battle at dawn Jackson muttered to his companion "Delicious excitement!"; and Lee, surveying a field of carnage, observed reflectively, "It is well that war is so horrible—we would grow too fond of it." Against Lee and his great lieutenant, united for a year of intense action in a comradeship which recalls that of Marlborough and Eugene, were now to be marshalled the overwhelming forces of the Union.

*   *   *   *   *

Both sides set to work to form armies. Trained officers and men were few, weapons and munitions scanty. The American people had enjoyed a long peace, and their warfare had been to reclaim the wilderness and draw wealth from the soil. On neither side was there any realisation of the ordeal that lay before them. The warlike spirit ran high in the South, and their gentry and frontier farmers, like the Cavaliers, were more accustomed to riding and shooting than their compeers in the commercial North. The Confederate states were defending hearth and home against invasion and overlordship. Proud and ardent, their manhood rallied to the newly forming regiments, confident that they would conquer, sure at least that they were unconquerable.

The North was at first astonished at the challenge. They could hardly realise that the wordy strife of party politics, the exciting turmoil of electioneering, must now give place to organised slaughter. When they surveyed the vast resources of the North they felt their power incomparable. All were resolved to maintain the Union whatever the cost; and beneath this august constitutional issue there glowed the moral fires of wrath against slavery.

At first sight, to foreign observers, the disparity between the combatants was evident. Twenty-three states, with a population of twenty-two millions, were arrayed against eleven states, whose population of nine millions included nearly four million slaves. But as the Southern states only claimed the right to go their own way their policy would be defensive; the North, which denied this right and was determined to keep them in the Union by force, had to take the offensive. A formidable task confronted the aggressors.

Nothing short of the subjugation of the entire South would suffice. The issue was not to be settled by two or three battles; the whole country would have to be conquered piecemeal. The Confederacy embraced an area which extended eight hundred miles from north to south and seventeen hundred from east to west. The railways were few and badly conditioned; the roads no better. The region was sparsely inhabited, and the invader would have for the most part to bring his own supplies. He would have enormously long lines of communication to guard in his march through a hostile country. Most of the slaves, who might have been expected to prove an embarrassment to the South, on the contrary proved a solid help, tending the plantations in the absence of their masters, raising the crops which fed the armies, working on the roads and building fortifications, thus releasing a large number of whites for service in the field.

In the North it might be suggested that a large proportion of the Democrats would oppose a policy of force. In the struggle of endurance, which seemed the shape which the war would ultimately take, the South might prove more staunch. In a war of attrition the North had the advantage of being a manufacturing community, and her best weapon against Southern agricultural strength, if it could blockade three thousand five hundred miles of Southern coast, might prove to be the Navy. But a resultant cotton famine in Europe might force Great Britain and France into intervention on the side of the South.

The seven states of the Lower South had seceded after Lincoln's election, and set up a Government of their own at Montgomery, Alabama, in February 1861. Lincoln's call for troops after Sumter was followed by the secession of four states of the Upper South, and the Confederate capital was moved to Richmond. There remained the attitude of the border slave states, Kentucky, Missouri, Maryland, and Delaware. Of these Kentucky was the most important on account of its geographical position, and because Missouri was likely to follow its example. Indeed, the issue of the war seemed perhaps to turn upon Kentucky. Lincoln, a Kentuckian by birth, like Jefferson Davis, is reported to have said, "I should like to have God on my side, but I must have Kentucky." But

Kentucky, loyal to the memory of Henry Clay, "the Great Compromiser," tried to remain neutral. Neither combatant could tolerate this attitude for long; yet both feared lest any violent act of aggression might throw the state into the other's arms. Lincoln proved the more astute diplomatist, and by keeping the control of policy in his own hands secured Kentucky for the Union in September. This was the first real victory for the North.

In Missouri, as in the sister state, there was a majority in favour of neutrality; but the extremists on both sides took control and civil war resulted. The Governor was a rabid Secessionist, and, supported by the legislature, endeavoured to take the state out of the Union. The Union leader was one of the powerful Blair family, and his brother a member of the Cabinet. He invoked the aid of General Lyon, commander of the Federal troops in St Louis, and with his help the Governor's separatist designs were defeated, and he himself chased out of Jefferson City, the state capital, into the south-west corner of the state. But the intrusion of Federal troops into a domestic quarrel caused many citizens who had hitherto been neutral to join the ranks of Secession. Although a state Convention deposed the Governor and set up a Provisional Government at St Louis months were to elapse before Missouri was fully brought under Federal control.

In Maryland the issue was more quickly settled. The Secessionists were strong in Baltimore, and gained temporary control of the city. They destroyed the railway bridges on the two northern lines, and for a few days Washington found itself dangerously isolated. Reinforcements from Massachusetts were assaulted in their march through the streets, and a bloody collision occurred. But without help from Virginia the Maryland Secessionists were not capable of making head against the national capital, and the Loyalist Governor gained time, until on May 13 General Butler, with a small Federal force, made a sudden dash, and, taking the Secessionists by surprise, occupied Baltimore. This ended the secession in Maryland. A fourth slave state, Delaware, also stayed in the Union. Its Legislature had Southern leanings, but geography ruled otherwise.

Lincoln not only secured four slavery states as allies, but also detached an important section from the seceding state of Virginia. West Virginia, separated by the Alleghenies from the rest of the state, and geographically and economically a part of the Ohio valley, had long chafed under the oppression of the state Government at Richmond, which ignored its interests and exploited it for the benefit of the "Tidewater" section. It now seized the opportunity to secede from Secession. When in May the popular vote ratified the Ordinance of Secession it broke away, and with the help of its powerful neighbour, Ohio, established its independence under the title of the state of Kanawha, which two years later was formally admitted to the Union as the state of West Virginia.

In the task of preparing for war the Southern President had advantages over his rival. A West-Pointer, he had served in the Regular Army for several years and had fought in the Mexican War; he had afterwards been Secretary of War in President Pierce's administration, and then chairman of the Senate Military Affairs Committee. He had an inside knowledge of the officer corps, and could make the best use of the material at his disposal. Not only did he select with a few exceptions the right men, but he supported them in adversity. The principal Confederate Generals who were in command at the beginning of the war, if not killed, were still in command at its end.

Lincoln, on the other hand, was without military experience; his profession of the law had not brought him in contact with Army officers. His appointments were too often made on purely political grounds. He was too ready, especially at first, to yield to the popular clamour which demanded the recall of an unsuccessful general. Few, having failed once, were given a second chance. After each defeat a change was made in the command of the Army of the Potomac. None of the Generals in command of Federal armies at the end of the war had held high commands at the beginning. The survivors were very good, but the Federal cause was the poorer for the loss of those who had fallen by the way. Others, fearing the President in the rear more than the foe in front, had been too nervous to fight their best. Nor did the War Department make the best use of the junior officers of the Regular Army. Too many were left with their detachments in the Far West instead of being utilised to train and lead the volunteers. But while the North attempted at first to organise its military strength as if it had been a confederacy of states, the Federal Government, gaining power steadily at the expense of the states, rapidly won unquestioned control over all the forces of the Union. The Southern "Sovereign States," on the other hand, were unable even under the stress of war to abandon the principle of decentralisation for which they had been contending. Some State Governors, though loyal to the Confederate cause, were slow to respond to central direction, and when conscription was decided upon by the Confederate Congress in 1862 there was much opposition and evasion by the state authorities.

*   *   *   *   *

By what paths should the North invade the South to reconquer it for the Union? The Allegheny Mountains divided the Mississippi valley from the broad slopes which stretched eastward to the Atlantic. The Mississippi and its great tributary, the Ohio, with the Cumberland and the Tennessee Rivers, offered sure means of carrying the war into the heart of the Confederacy and rending it asunder. The mechanical and material resources of the North ensured the control of these waterways. The South could not organise any river forces capable of coping with the Federal flotillas. The one lateral line of communication within Confederate territory, the Charleston–Memphis railroad, which passed through the key position of Chattanooga on the Tennessee, at the junction of four railway lines, would be speedily threatened. Waterways could not be cut by cavalry raids; the current of the rivers was with the North, and there was no limit except shipping to the troops and the supplies which could be carried. Old Winfield Scott, the Federal General-in-Chief, saw in this Western theatre the true line of strategic advance. But the initial neutrality of Kentucky confused the Northern view, and when at the end of September Kentucky was gained the main Union forces were differently engaged.

Upon Virginia joining the Confederacy Jefferson Davis made Richmond the Southern capital. It was within a hundred miles of Washington. It controlled, or might control, the estuaries of the James and York Rivers, with their tributaries. It covered the powerful naval base at Norfolk. Between Richmond and the enemy flowed in successive barriers the broad outlets of the Potomac and the Rappahannock, with its tributary the Rapidan. Here, then, upon this advanced battleground, rather than in the interior, must the Confederacy maintain itself or fall. Thus the two capitals stood like queens at chess upon adjoining squares, and, sustained by their combinations of covering pieces, they endured four years of grim play within a single move of capture.

The Confederates hoped at first to defend the line of the Potomac, which marked the northern frontier of Virginia. They had seized the Federal arsenal and army depot at Harpers Ferry, where the Shenandoah joins the Potomac, and for several months, while the Union forces were gathering, Colonel Jackson, and later General Joseph E. Johnston, with a few thousand men, maintained themselves there. In front of the railway junction of Manassas, by the Bull Run stream, only thirty miles from Washington, stood General Beauregard, of Sumter repute, with the main Confederate army. Thus the summer of 1861 came. "How long," cried the politicians in Washington, and the turbulent public opinion behind them in the North, "should the United States tolerate this insolent challenge?" The three-months volunteers whom Lincoln had summoned at the end of April must be made to strike a blow before their time expired. General Scott wished to wait till trained armies were formed. But do not all regulars despise militia and volunteers? Pressed beyond resistance, Scott yielded to the entreaties of Lincoln and his Cabinet. Harpers Ferry had already been recovered, and Joseph E. Johnston, with eleven thousand men, had withdrawn up the Shenandoah, Scott therefore sent fifteen thousand men to hold off Johnston in the valley, while Irvin McDowell, a competent soldier, with thirty-five thousand, moved to attack Beauregard, who mustered twenty-two thousand. The essence of this plan was that Johnston's army, held by superior force, should not join Beauregard before McDowell attacked him. Some have suggested that if Scott, who was still robust of mind, if not in body, could have been conveyed to the field of battle in a litter or ambulance, as Marshal Saxe had been at Fontenoy, the Federal army might have been spared the disaster which overtook it. Knowledge and experience in command outweigh mere physical disability.

The Federal advance had originally been fixed for July 9, but it was not till a week later that it actually began. The two Confederate Generals were both expecting to be attacked by the superior forces on their respective fronts, and each was asking for reinforcements from the other. But the Union General in the valley, Patterson, allowed Johnston to slip away unobserved, and he joined Beauregard with two brigades on the day before the battle. Both McDowell and Beauregard had planned the same manœuvre, to turn the enemy's left flank. McDowell got his blow in first; on the Confederate right orders miscarried and the offensive faltered. With such troops the side standing on the defensive might be expected to hold its ground. But McDowell virtually achieved a surprise, and his much superior force threatened to overwhelm the weak Confederate left before reinforcements could arrive. In this crisis Jackson's brigade, standing "like a stone wall" on the Henry Hill, stopped the Federal advance, until the arrival by rail of another of Johnston's brigades turned the tide of battle.

The combat, though fierce, was confused, and on both sides disjointed. The day was hot, the troops raw, the staffs inexperienced. The Northerners retreated; the Confederates were too disorganised to pursue; but the retreat became a rout. Members of the Cabinet, Senators, Congressmen, even ladies, had come out from Washington to see the sport. They were involved in a panic when thousands of men, casting away their arms and even their coats, fled and never stopped till they reached the entrenchments which surrounded Washington. Not more than five thousand men were killed or wounded on both sides in the action, but the name Bull Run rang far and wide. Europe was astonished; the South was overjoyed; and a wave of fury swept the Union, before which the passions which had followed the attack on Fort Sumter seemed but a ripple.

It is still argued that the Confederates should have struck hot-foot at Washington. But Johnston at the time thought the

Confederate army more disorganised by victory than the Federals by defeat. He had not seen the rout. Jackson and other Confederate Generals were eager to advance on Washington. Who shall say?

*　　*　　*　　*　　*

The day after this ignominious affair a new commander replaced McDowell. One of Lee's comrades on Scott's staff in Mexico, General George B. McClellan, a Regular officer with many remarkable qualities, was summoned from West Virginia, where he had been active and forward, to take command. Congress had voted the enlistment of five hundred thousand volunteers and a grant of two hundred and fifty million dollars for the prosecution of the war. A week after his assumption of command McClellan laid before the President the grandiose scheme of forming an army of two hundred and seventy-three thousand men, which, in combination with a strong naval force and a fleet of transports, should march through the Atlantic states, reducing the seaports from Richmond to New Orleans, and then move into the interior and stamp out the remnants of the rebellion. In war matters are not settled so easily. Public opinion, vocal through a thousand channels, demanded quick results. The scythe of Time cut both ways. The Confederacy was becoming consolidated. Every month increased the peril of foreign recognition of the South, or even of actual intervention. However, when at the end of October General Scott retired McClellan became General-in-Chief of all the armies of the Republic, and bent himself with zeal and capacity to forming brigades, divisions, army corps, with artillery, engineers, and supply trains, according to the best European models.

The year 1861 ended with the Confederacy intact and almost unmolested. Along the immense front, with its deep borderlands and debatable regions, more than a hundred and

GENERAL JOSEPH ("FIGHTING JOE") HOOKER
Appointed Commander-in-Chief of the Army of the Potomac, January 26, 1863

THE BATTLE OF CHANCELLORSVILLE

The stonewall at the foot of Marye's Heights, Fredericksburg, scene of Sedgwick's charge against the Confederate position on May 3, 1863

THE BATTLE OF GETTYSBURG

Confederate sniper killed in "Devil's Den" by shellfire during the four days' battle of July 1863

The battlefield on July 4. The lines of dead of the Federal 24th Michigan Infantry

FORT SUMTER

The scene of a night attack by Federal troops on September 8, 1863 fifty skirmishes and petty actions had been fought without serious bloodshed. Although the Confederate commanders realised that the time would soon come when McClellan would take the field against them with an army vastly superior in numbers, well disciplined and well equipped, they did not dare, with only forty thousand men, however elated, to invade Maryland and march on Baltimore. They did not even attempt to recover West Virginia. Lee, who was sent to co-ordinate defence on this front, could not prevail over the discord of the local commanders. Although he still retained his commission from the state of Virginia, he ranked below both Joseph E. Johnston and Albert Sidney Johnston in the Confederate hierarchy. Beauregard, though junior to him, had gained the laurels. Lee returned from Western Virginia with diminished reputation, and President Davis had to explain his qualities to the State Governors when appointing him to organise the coast defences of the Carolinas.

So far the American Civil War had appeared to Europe as a desultory brawl of mobs and partisans which might at any time be closed by politics and parley. Napoleon III sympathised with the Confederates, and would have aided them if the British Government had been agreeable. Queen Victoria desired a strict neutrality, and opinion in England was curiously divided. The upper classes, Conservative and Liberal alike, generally looked with favour upon the South, and in this view Gladstone concurred. Disraeli, the Conservative leader, was neutral. The Radicals and the unenfranchised mass of the working classes were solid against slavery, and Cobden and Bright spoke their mind. But the Northern blockade struck hard at the commercial classes, and Lancashire, though always constant against slavery, began to feel the cotton famine. The arrest on a British ship, the *Trent,* of the Confederate agents, Mason and Slidell, by a United States cruiser roused a storm. The Foreign Secretary, Lord John Russell, penned a hard dispatch which the Prince Consort persuaded the Prime Minister, Lord Palmerston, to modify. A clause was inserted which enabled the Federal Government without loss of honour to declare their cruiser's action unauthorised. President Lincoln took some persuading, but in the end he sagely remarked "One war at a time," liberated the captives, and all remained in sullen suspense. Blockade-running, both in cotton outwards and arms inwards, developed upon a large scale; but not a single European Government received the envoys of the Confederate states. No one in Europe imagined the drama of terrific war which the year 1862 would unfold. None appraised truly the implacable rage of the antagonists. None understood the strength of Abraham Lincoln or the resources of the United States. Few outside the Confederacy had ever heard of Lee or Jackson.

CHAPTER FOUR

The Campaign Against Richmond

THE New Year opened grievously for the South, and a bitter tide of disillusion chilled its people. In the Cabinet and headquarters at Richmond, where facts and figures told their sombre tale, the plight of the Confederacy already seemed grave. The Union blockade froze the coasts. Hostile armies, double or triple the numbers the South could muster, were assuming shape and quality, both in the Atlantic and Mississippi theatres. The awful weight of the North, with its wealth and munition-making power, lay now upon the minds of President Davis, his colleagues and Generals. The Southern states had no arsenals, little iron and steel, few and small factories from which boots, clothing, equipment could be supplied. The magazines were almost empty. Even flintlock muskets were scarce. The smooth-bore cannon of the Confederate artillery was far out-ranged by the new rifled guns of the Union. Nor was there any effectual means by which these needs could be met. It is upon this background that the military prodigies of the year stand forth.

Disaster opened in the Mississippi valley. Here Albert Sidney Johnston commanded the Confederate forces. Davis believed him to be his finest General. He was certainly a man of boundless devotion, whose daring was founded upon a thorough knowledge of his art. In the autumn of 1861 he had

advanced to Bowling Green, a railway junction of high strategic value to the south of the Green River, a tributary of the
Ohio. Here he stood brazenly, hoping to rouse Kentucky and
marshal Tennessee, while to the westward Leonidas Polk,
who in peace-time was Bishop of Louisiana, with another
small army barred the Mississippi at Columbus. The Federal
forces, with their fleets of armoured river gun-boats, descend-
ing the Mississippi from St Louis and the Ohio from Louisville, outnumbered both these Confederate Generals by four
to one. Still, for months they had remained unmolested in
their forward positions, covering enormous territories from
whose population and resources much might be drawn. Now
with the turn of the year the Union leaders set their men in
motion. Masses of blue-clad soldiers began to appear upon
the three-hundred-mile front from the great river to the
mountain ranges, and all kinds of queer craft cased in steel
and carrying cannon and mortars glided slowly down the riv-
erways from the north. The bluff could be played no longer.
Polk abandoned Columbus, and Johnston retreated from
Bowling Green. This carried the fighting line southwards to
the Cumberland and Tennessee Rivers, and to a Confederate
fortress called Island No. 10 on the Mississippi.

The Federal General, Henry W. Halleck, who commanded
the Western Department was a model of caution. Fortunately
among his generals there was a retired Regular officer, Ulysses S. Grant, who since the Mexican War had lived in ob-
scurity, working for a time in his father's leather store in
Illinois. The Confederates sought to block the Mississippi at
Island No. 10, the Tennessee at Fort Henry, and the Cumberland at Fort Donelson, and their advanced forces garri-
soned these armed posts. Fort Henry was weak, and Fort
Donelson was an entrenched camp which required a considerable army for its defence. Grant proposed a winter advance

up the Tennessee River and an attack upon Fort Henry. Halleck approved. Grant made the advance, and the advance made Grant. Albert Sidney Johnston foresaw with perfect clarity a Federal winter offensive while the rivers were well filled. He clamoured for reinforcements, both to President Davis and the Governors of the Western states. The former could not and the latter did not supply them. In February 1862 Grant seized Fort Henry. It was but ten miles across the tongue of land between the rivers to Fort Donelson, on the Cumberland. Without authority, and in severe frost, Grant struck at Fort Donelson, which was defended by seventeen thousand Confederates under Floyd, the former United States Secretary for War, who in the interval between Lincoln's election and inauguration had allowed the muskets to be transferred to the South. After four days' fighting and confrontation Fort Donelson surrendered, with fourteen thousand prisoners and sixty guns. Floyd, apprehending a charge of treason, escaped the night before. He was probably wise.

The fall of Fort Donelson on February 16 was the first great military disaster of the Confederacy; but others followed quickly in the West. Albert Sidney Johnston, now at last furnished with the beginnings of an army, gathered the remnants of his former front at Corinth, behind the Tennessee, and Polk fell back down the Mississippi to Memphis.

* * * * *

At Washington McClellan, General-in-Chief, laboured to prepare his army, and resisted by every means the intense political pressures which demanded an advance "on to Richmond." He exaggerated the strength of the enemy, and furnished Lincoln with endless reports from Pinkerton's Private Detective Agency, which he used as his secret service, showing very heavy forces at Richmond and behind Joseph E. Johnston's entrenchments thirty miles away at Centerville.

He strove to gain time to drill his men by repeated promises to advance. As month succeeded month and the swarming Army of the Potomac made no movement the enthusiasm which had greeted McClellan in July 1861 waned. The Radical Republicans began to attack this Democrat General who had been preferred to their own candidate, John C. Frémont. McClellan was known to be opposed to the Radical policy of proclaiming the emancipation of all slaves. Early in December he informed the President that he did not favour a frontal attack on Joseph E. Johnston and a march along the straight road through Fredericksburg to Richmond. He had long been devising a plan for an amphibious movement down Chesapeake Bay to some point on the coast of Virginia close to the rebel capital. He imparted these ideas to Lincoln in general terms early in December. Then in the middle of the month he contracted typhoid fever and was absent for several weeks. The Republican Party leaders had already procured the appointment of a Joint Committee on the conduct of the war, consisting of three Senators and four Congressmen. It was dominated by the Radical enemies of the General-in-Chief. Lincoln and the cabinet, during McClellan's absence from duty, called into council several Generals of the Army, and invited constructive suggestions. But their conferences were abruptly disturbed by the reappearance of McClellan himself. A few days later he explained his plan to the President in detail. Availing himself of sea-power, he proposed to transport an army of a hundred and fifty thousand men down Chesapeake Bay and disembark it at Urbana, on the Lower Rappahannock, where it would be only one day's march from West Point and two more marches from Richmond. He expected to cut off General J. B. Magruder and the Confederate troops defending the Yorktown peninsula, and he hoped to reach Richmond before Johnston could retreat thither.

No one can asperse the principle of this conception. It utilised all the forces of the Union Government; it turned the flank of all the Confederate positions between Washington and Richmond; it struck at the forehead of the Confederacy. Its details were substantially modified on examination. Fortress Monroe, at the tip of the peninsula, between the York and James Rivers, was held by the Union, and was finally chosen as a safe landing-place. President Lincoln had one overpowering objection to the whole idea of a maritime expedition. It would uncover Washington; and Joseph E. Johnston, for the strength of whose army he probably accepted McClellan's own figures, to say nothing of "Stonewall" Jackson, would at once swoop down on the defenceless capital. Hard bargaining ensued upon the number of troops to be left to guard the capital and the mouth of the Shenandoah valley, where at Harpers Ferry the river flows into the Potomac. This was agreed at forty thousand. Eventually on February 27 Lincoln gave a reluctant assent, and everything was set in train for the tremendous enterprise. At the same time Lincoln resolved to keep supreme control, relieved McClellan of the general direction of the United States armies, and restricted him to the command of the Army of the Potomac. For this there were also sound military reasons. Feeling that he required a military adviser, he decided to summon General Halleck from the West. McClellan learnt of his removal from the higher command through the medium of the newspapers before Lincoln's emissary reached him. Thus the President appeared guilty of a grave discourtesy, so unusual in him that the suspicion naturally arose that the "hidden hand" of the Joint Committee was here at work.

It was a far worse mistake not to appoint a new General-in-Chief. All the generals in command of armies were ordered to take their instructions from the Secretary of War. For the last two months this office had been held by Edwin M. Stanton, who had replaced the incompetent and perhaps corrupt Cameron. Stanton, like McClellan, was a Democrat, and during the last days of the Buchanan administration had held the post of Attorney-General. Possibly Lincoln thought that he would be acceptable to McClellan. It was no doubt his intention to reappoint McClellan as General-in-Chief, if he succeeded in his Richmond campaign, and at the time he could think of no one to fill the vacancy, which he hoped would be only temporary. At the outset Stanton had professed unbounded devotion to McClellan, but the General soon began to doubt the sincerity of his professions and thought that he detected a deliberate design to debar him from free access to the President. It was not very long before Stanton appeared to be in collusion with the Joint Committee. The Attorney-General had given the opinion that "the order of the Secretary of War is the President's order." There now began to issue from the Secretary's office a series of orders seriously crippling McClellan's operations. McClellan's scope was reduced by the creation of the Military Departments of the Rappahannock under McDowell, who had commanded at Bull Run, and of the Shenandoah under Nathaniel P. Banks. A whole corps was thus taken from him. He claimed that he was leaving behind him no less than seventy-three thousand men, of whom but thirty-five thousand belonged to Banks's command in the Shenandoah valley. McClellan was justified in regarding this force as available for the protection of the capital. However, he did not clearly explain his arrangements to Lincoln, and his failure to take the President into his confidence had an unfortunate result. For Lincoln in misunderstanding ordered the First Corps, under McDowell, to remain in front of Washington, thus reducing the force on which McClellan had counted by forty thousand men, at the moment of launching his tremendous operation.

*　　*　　*　　*　　*

The Confederates lost their best chance of victory when they failed to use the autumn and winter of 1861. Their success at Bull Run proved as injurious as a reverse. Believing with their President that foreign intervention was near at hand, and arrogantly confident that they could beat the North in the field if need arose, they relaxed their efforts. The volunteers who came forward after the first battle could not be armed. Recruiting fell off; the soldiers in the field began to go home. Efforts to fill the ranks by grants of bounties and furloughs were ineffectual. By the beginning of 1862 the position was desperate. Nearly two-thirds of the Confederate Army consisted of one-year volunteers. In May the terms of enlistment of the hundred and forty-eight regiments which they formed would expire. These regiments were the backbone of the Army. Invasion was imminent. Conscription was contrary to the theory of state independence and sovereignty. But the Confederate Congress rose manfully to the occasion, and on April 16 by a vote of more than two to one passed an Act declaring every able-bodied white man between the ages of eighteen and thirty-five subject to military service. The armies were nevertheless filled by volunteers seeking to escape the stigma of serving under compulsion rather than by the Act itself. Indeed, the Act proved unpopular in the States and was difficult to enforce. Full use was made of its exemption clauses by the disaffected in order to escape service.

Throughout this period President Jefferson Davis rigorously adhered to the passive-defensive. He made no attempt to exploit the victories of Bull Run and Wilson's Creek. Determined to keep the control of military operations in his own hands, he devoted his attention to the East, and largely ignored the West, where chaos reigned until Albert Sidney Johnston's appointment to the supreme command in September. He obstinately refused to draw upon the "seasoned soldiers" who formed the garrisons on the Atlantic coastline. Hatteras Inlet, which afforded the best approach to the North Carolina Sounds, and Port Royal and Beaufort in South Carolina, which threatened both Charleston and Savannah, had been captured by small Federal forces and sea-power. Lee after his return from Western Virignia was sent to organise the coast defences. When a large expedition under the Union General Ambrose E. Burnside entered the inland waters of North Carolina the Confederates were ill-prepared, and lost Roanoke Island and New Bern. President Davis was more than ever determined to maintain at their full strength the garrisons in the threatened states. He recalled General Lee from his coastal defence work in the Carolinas, and employed him in a somewhat ill-defined capacity as his chief military adviser at headquarters.

In the middle of March Halleck, who had been appointed to the sole command in the Western theatre, directed Don Carlos Buell, who had occupied Nashville, to march with the greater part of his army to Savannah, on the Tennessee, thirty miles from Corinth, to combine with Grant, who had William T. Sherman with him, on the western bank near Shiloh, and attack Albert Sidney Johnston. But before Buell's men were across the river Johnston struck. In the early morning of April 6 he surprised the advanced Federal troops in their tents near Shiloh, and the largest and most bloody battle yet seen in the war was fought. Johnston at first carried all before him; and Grant, who was late in reaching the field, was by nightfall in grave danger. But Johnston, exposing himself with reckless gallantry at the head of an infantry charge, was wounded and bled to death from a main artery in a few minutes. Whatever results his great personality and wonderful energy could have gained on the morrow were lost. Beauregard, who succeeded him, drew off the Confederate troops, much to the disgust of his subordinate, Braxton Bragg. Each side lost in this furious action ten thousand men; but the proportion of loss was far heavier in the thinner Confederate ranks. The arrival of the cautious Halleck, although he brought Federal reinforcements, stopped any thought of pursuit. Island No. 10 was reduced by General John Pope on April 8, and seven thousand Confederates became prisoners of war. It now seems that a combined naval and military expedition could easily at this time have lunged far to the south and secured the fortress of Vicksburg in Mississippi. But Halleck accommodated himself readily to the President's wish for action in East Tennessee. He moved slowly against Corinth, and spent a month in trying to surround Beauregard, who escaped by a swift and long retreat. By the summer the Union line in the West had moved southwards by two hundred miles on a three-hundred-mile front.

* * * * *

The stage was now set for the military drama of the Richmond-Yorktown peninsula. At the beginning of April McClellan's army began to land in large numbers at the Federal Fortress Monroe, which served as a bridgehead. As soon as this movement, about which there could be no secrecy, became evident Joseph E. Johnston, to the surprise and relief of the Federal Government, withdrew from Centreville, abandoned Manassas Junction, crossed the Upper Rappahannock, and stood in the rugged wilderness country behind its tributary the Rapidan. It may seem confusing that there should be two Confederate Generals named Johnston; but after the gallant death of Albert Sidney at Shiloh only one remained.

He was Joseph E. Now behind the Rapidan he was in close touch with Richmond, so that McClellan's strategy, vindicated in principle, was baulked in practice. In the middle of April Johnston, leaving his main army eighty miles to the westward, arrived at Yorktown, and assumed the additional command of the troops in the peninsula. He thus enjoyed interior lines and could concentrate all his forces for the defence of Richmond. The Union Navy, after a heavy combat, found itself unable to face the plunging fire of the batteries on the bluffs of the York River on McClellan's right flank. The Confederate entrenchments, manned by Magruder's troops, stretched before him across the peninsula. He conceived himself outnumbered by the enemy, and if Davis had consented to give Johnston the garrisons of the Atlantic towns he would have been.

In these depressing circumstances McClellan acted with more than his habitual deliberation. He spent a month in a formal siege of Yorktown, incessantly appealing to Lincoln for McDowell's corps. Lincoln, on the other hand, urged him to vigorous action. "I always insisted," he wrote drily, on April 9, "that going down the bay in search of a field instead of fighting at or near Manassas was only shifting and not surmounting a difficulty; that we would find the same enemy, and the same or equal entrenchments, at either place." And a month later: "By delay the enemy will relatively gain upon you—that is, he will gain faster by fortifications and reinforcements than you can gain by reinforcements alone." Eventually, after the surrender of Yorktown, which opened the York River to his ships, McClellan advanced upon the Confederate lines. Magruder, who had only eleven thousand men, made no resistance, and though mauled in a rearguard action at Williamsburg on May 5 extricated himself successfully. By the middle of May McClellan had advanced sixty miles up the York, and arrived at White House, on the Richmond—

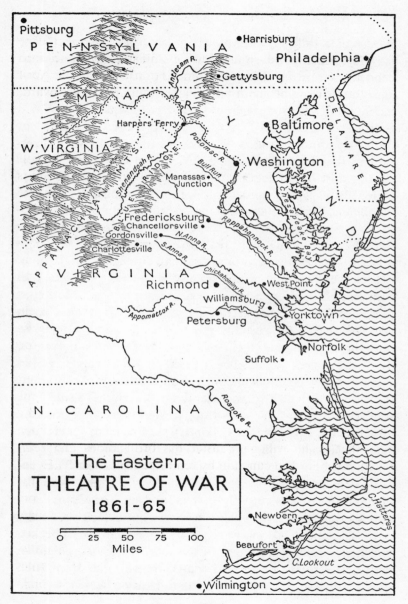

The Eastern
THEATRE OF WAR
1861-65

0   25   50   75   100
Miles

West Point railway, twenty-five miles from the rebel capital. He formed a new base at West Point and became independent of Fortress Monroe. Could he at this moment have brought McDowell from Fredericksburg into his combination the fate of Richmond might well have been sealed.

However, President Davis had in April been persuaded by Lee to reinforce "Stonewall" Jackson for an offensive diversion in the Shenandoah valley. With only sixteen thousand men against four Federal Generals, Banks, Shields, Frémont and Milroy, who disposed of over forty thousand, Jackson fought the brief, brilliant campaign which reinforced his first renown. Striking right and left at the superior forces on either side of him, running daily risks of capture, making enormous marches, sometimes dividing his small force, he gained a series of sharp actions, which greatly perturbed President Lincoln and his advisers. Lincoln had at last promised McClellan McDowell's corps; but six days later, when the Union Army was half across the swampy river Chickahominy, a telegram brought the General the news that McDowell's movement was "suspended." McClellan paused in his advance; violent rains flooded the Chickahominy, and the Union Army found itself divided, with two corps only on the southern side. This was clearly Johnston's opportunity. With his whole force he attacked the two isolated Union corps. President Davis, with Lee at his side, rode out to watch the resulting battle of Seven Pines, or Fair Oaks as it is sometimes called. They had not been consulted by the Commander-in-Chief, who had given all his orders verbally to his Generals. The Confederate attack miscarried. The battle was severe but indecisive, costing each side about six thousand men. McClellan was checked, and heavy rains made him all the more ready to remain inactive. He stood fast with his outposts five miles from Richmond. Lincoln, having learned that Jackson was now in retreat up the valley, again promised McDowell's corps. But when Jackson turned on his pursuers and defeated them on two successive days, June 8 and 9, at Cross Keys and Port Republic, he changed his mind again and would not let Mc-Dowell go. It was certainly desirable to guard against any risk of the Federal capital's falling even temporarily into rebel hands, for the effect would have been shattering, though hardly disastrous. But Lincoln's vacillations are a classic instance of the dangers of civilian interference with generals in the field.

Far more important than the fighting was the fact that General Joseph E. Johnston was severely wounded on the first day at Seven Pines, and President Davis on June 1 appointed Lee to command what was henceforward to bear the deathless title of the Army of Northern Virginia.

* * * * *

Lee now made the first of his offensive combinations, and immediately his hand was felt in the whole conduct of the war. He procured from Davis the gathering of the Atlantic garrisons which Johnston had been denied. He played upon the fears of Washington by sending seven thousand men to strengthen Jackson in the valley. This ensured the further paralysis of McDowell. Jackson rode in from his army to concert the plans. He was ordered to leave his "enfeebled troops" in the valley, and come secretly with his main force to Ashland, fifteen miles north of Richmond and on the Richmond–Fredericksburg railway. He could thence by advancing turn the flank and the rear of the Union armies and cut their communications with West Point. He was to be ready to act by dawn on June 26. In the interval J. E. B. Stuart, the young Confederate cavalry leader, with twelve hundred horse, made a remarkable reconnaissance of McClellan's right. He actually traversed his communications, and, being unable to return, rode right round the Union Army, arriving south of Richmond with several hundred captives. This was more than Lee had wished, and Stuart's exploit might well have warned the enemy. But McClellan made no change in his array, which still lay in sight of Richmond astride the Chickahominy. Lee's army, counting Jackson, was now over seventy-five thousand strong. McClellan mustered eighty-seven thousand; but of these only the corps of General Fitz-John Porter, twenty-five thousand strong, was now north of the Chickahominy. Lee resolved to move the bulk of his force across that river, and, joined by Jackson, to concentrate fifty-six thousand men against Porter's corps, turn its right flank, destroy it, sever McClellan's communications with West Point, and thereafter cross the Chickahominy in his rear and bring him to ruin. There would be left in the entrenchments defending Richmond only sixteen thousand men under Magruder. It would be open to McClellan, when he saw what was afoot, to march with sixty thousand men straight upon the Richmond lines and assault them with a superiority of nearly four to one. Lee, who knew McClellan well, and judged him rightly, was sure he would not do this. "Anyhow," he said to Davis, "I shall be hard on his heels"—meaning that he would be attacking the Union Army from the rear while it was fighting its way into Richmond. This remark illustrates the agile, flexible grasp which Lee had of war, and how great commanders seem to move their armies from place to place as if they were doing no more than riding their own horses.

During the night of June 25 two Confederate corps crossed the Chickahominy, formed to their right, and fell upon Porter at Mechanicsville. Porter, surprised, made a stubborn resistance. His batteries of rifled cannon wrought havoc in the Confederate ranks. Jackson did not appear upon the scene. The difficulties of the route had delayed him by a day. Porter, hav-

ing inflicted a loss of over two thousand men upon his assailants, was able to fall back upon his reserves at Gaines's Mill,
four miles farther downstream, where the onslaught was renewed with the greatest fury on June 27. Gaines's Mill was
the first battle in which Lee commanded personally. It was
bitterly contested. Again the power of the Union artillery was
manifest. The Confederates were several times repulsed at
all points, and the country on Porter's right was so obstructed
with forest and swamp that when Jackson came into action
in the late afternoon he could not turn the flank. Lee however did not despair. He appealed to his troops. He launched
J. B. Hood's gallant Texans at the centre, and as the shadows
lengthened ordered the whole army to attack. The Texans
broke the centre of Porter's hard-tried corps. The Union
troops were driven from the field. Twenty guns and several
thousand prisoners were already taken when night fell. Where
would Porter go? McClellan had remained immobile opposite Magruder during the two days' fighting. What would he
do? His communications were cut. His right wing was crushed.
Lee's long, swinging left arm, of which Jackson was at last
the fist, must curve completely round the right and rear of
the Federal Army. Surely the stroke was mortal?

But McClellan was a skilful soldier. When his generals met
him at headquarters on the night of Gaines's Mill he informed
them that he had let go his communications with West Point
and the York River; that, using sea-power, he was shifting his
base from the York to the James; that the whole army would
march southwards to Harrison's Landing on that river, where
all supplies would await them. He had, we now know, made
some preparations for such a change beforehand. But he ran
a grave risk in leaving the decision till the last moment. What
was called, from its shape, a "grape-vine bridge" had been
built across the swamps and stream of the Chickahominy,

and by this tortuous, rickety structure Porter made good his escape, while the whole Federal Army prepared to make a difficult and dangerous flank march across the White Oak Swamp to the southern side of the peninsula. It was now Magruder's turn to advance and strike at this vulnerable army. He broke in upon them on the 28th at Savage Station, capturing their field hospitals and large supplies. But Lee could not yet be sure that McClellan was really making for the James. He might as well be retreating by the Williamsburg road on Fortress Monroe. Lee therefore delayed one day before crossing the Chickahominy in pursuit. It was not till the 30th that he brought McClellan to battle at Glendale, or Frayser's Farm. This was the main crisis.

It is almost incredible that McClellan spent the day conferring with the Navy and arranging the new base on the James. He left the battle to fight itself. On the Confederate side many things went wrong. The maps were faulty; the timing failed; the attacks were delivered piecemeal; Jackson, from whom so much had been hoped, appeared in physical eclipse. Out of seventy-five thousand men with whom Lee had proposed to deal the final blow barely twenty thousand were really launched. These, after frightful losses, broke the Union centre; but night enabled the army to continue its retreat. At Malvern Hill, in a position of great strength, with the James River behind them to forbid further retreat, and the fire of the Navy and its gunboats to cover their flanks, McClellan stood at bay. Once again at the end of this week of furious fighting Lee ordered the attack, and his soldiers charged with their marvellous impetuosity. Loud roared the Union cannonade; high rose the rebel yell, that deadly sound *"Aah-ih!"* so often to be heard in these bloody years. But all was in vain. McClellan was saved. Frustrated, beaten, driven into retreat, his whole campaign wrecked, with a loss of enormous masses of stores and munitions, sixty cannon and thirty-six thousand rifles, with Richmond invincible, McClellan and his brave army nevertheless finished the Battle of the Seven Days by hurling back their pursuers with the loss of five thousand men.

Victory in the Seven Days' Battle rested with Lee. The world saw the total failure of the immense Federal plan. This also was the impression at Washington. McClellan, who was undaunted, proposed to move across the James to Petersburg and attack Richmond "by the back door," as Grant was to do in 1865. His proposals were not accepted. But to Lee the adventure was hardly less disappointing. He had failed by a succession of narrow chances, arising largely from the newness of his staffs, to annihilate his foe. He had lost over twenty thousand of the flower of his army, against seventeen thousand on the Union side with its overflowing man-power.

Lincoln and his advisers now sought to return to their original plan of massing overwhelming forces on the overland route between Washington and Richmond and breaking through by weight of numbers. But their armies were divided, and Lee at Richmond stood directly between them. The President ordered McClellan to withdraw from the peninsula and bring his troops up the Potomac to the neighbourhood of Washington. Halleck, who was then credited with the successes gained against his orders in the Western theatre, was appointed General-in-Chief. He brought General Pope, who had done well in the Mississippi valley, to command what was to be called "the Army of Virginia." Pope was a harsh, vainglorious man, puffed up with good fortune in the Western theatre, and speaking in derogatorty terms of the armies of the East and their achievements. He would show them how war should be waged. McClellan was ordered to hand over his troops, who parted from him in outspoken grief, and was relegated to the defence of the Washington lines. Pope now would be the champion of the Union. He signalised his appointment by severities upon the civil population of Western Virginia not yet used in the war. All male inhabitants in the zone of his army must either swear allegiance to the Union or be driven from their homes on pain of death if they returned. Jackson only with difficulty preserved his habitual calm on hearing this news about his beloved native state.

The strategic situation offered advantages to Lee and his lieutenant. Before McClellan's army could be brought round from the Yorktown peninsula they would deal with Pope. How they treated him must be recounted.

* * * * *

An historic naval episode had meanwhile occurred. When in the spring of 1861 the Federal Government had lightly abandoned the Navy yard at Norfolk to the seceding state of Virginia some stores and several vessels of the United States Navy had been burned. One of these, the frigate *Merrimac,* was repaired and refashioned in a curious way. It was given steam-engines to propel it, and above its deck a low penthouse of teak was erected. This was covered with two layers of railway iron hammered into two-inch plates. These layers were riveted transversely upon each other, making an ironclad shelter four inches thick. A heavy metal ram was fastened to the prow, and a battery of ten 7-inch rifled guns, firing through portholes, was mounted in the penthouse. Many had thought of this sort of thing before; now it came upon the scene.

This strange vessel was only finished on March 7, 1862. She had never fired a gun, nor had her engines been revolved, when on March 8 she went into action against the all-powerful Navy of the United States, which from Fortress Monroe was blockading the estuaries of the York and James Rivers.

The engines, described as the worst possible, were found to make only five knots an hour, and the vessel swam and steered like a waterlogged ship. Out she came, and with no hesitation engaged the two nearest ships of the blockading fleet, the *Cumberland* and the *Congress.* These delivered broadsides which would have sunk an ordinary frigate. Besides this, all other United States ships in range and the shore batteries at Sewell's Point concentrated their fire upon her. Without paying the slightest attention to this bombardment, the *Merrimac,* rechristened the *Virginia,* steered straight for the *Cumberland,* and struck her almost at right angles. On board the *Merrimac* the collision was hardly perceptible. The ram broke off; the *Cumberland* heeled over, and, firing her cannon to the last, soon foundered, with most of her crew. The *Merrimac* then turned upon the *Congress,* and at two hundred yards range smashed her to pieces and set her on fire. After an hour the *Congress* hoisted the white flag, and every effort was made by various small Confederate ships to rescue her crew. The *Minnesota,* which was aground, would have shared her fate if the ebb tide had not prevented the *Merrimac,* which drew twenty-two feet of water, from approaching her. Although the *Merrimac* was for a long time under the fire of at least a hundred heavy guns her armour was hardly damaged. Nothing outside the armour escaped. The funnel and two of the muzzles of the guns were shot off. Inside only twenty-one men were killed or wounded by splinters through the portholes. Her triumphant crew lay down by the side of their guns, expecting to destroy the rest of the United States fleet the next morning.

But when daylight came and steam was raised a strange-looking vessel was seen to be protecting the *Minnesota.* "She appeared," wrote one of the *Merrimac's* crew, "but a pigmy compared with the lofty frigate which she guarded." This was

Ericsson's *Monitor,* of which there had been much talk, now at last ready. The *Merrimac* had made the naval revolution, but the *Monitor,* one day later, was a whole lap ahead of her. She carried only two guns; but they were eleven-inch, and mounted in a revolving iron turret nine inches thick. She had a turtle deck, heavily protected, almost flush with the water-line. As she drew only twelve feet of water she had an advantage in manœuvre.

Both these ironclad monsters approached each other, while the stately ships of the United States fleet watched spellbound. They came to the closest quarters, and the *Merrimac,* now ramless, struck the *Monitor.* None of the *Merrimac's* shells pierced the *Monitor's* armour; but when the two eleven-inch guns hit the *Merrimac* amidships the whole side was driven in several inches, and all the guns' crews bled at the nose from concussion. For six hours these two ironclads battered each other with hardly any injury or loss on either side, and both withdrew at close of day, never to meet again. As the *Merrimac* had no armour below the water-line her crew considered her lucky. She returned to the dock-yard to have this defect and many others repaired. The *Monitor,* which was so unseaworthy that she had nearly foundered on the way to the fight, also required attention. As soon as the news reached Europe it was realised that all the war-fleets of the world were obsolete. The British Admiralty, by an intense effort, in the course of a few years reconstructed the Royal Navy so as to meet the altered conditions. But even now there are fools who build large ships to fight at sea with hardly any armour.[1] The combat of the *Merrimac* and the *Monitor* made the greatest change in sea-fighting since cannon fired by gunpowder had been mounted on ships about four hundred years before.

When Norfolk was evacuated by the Confederates efforts

[1] Written in 1939.

were made to take the *Merrimac* up the James River for the defence of Richmond; but although she was so lightened as to become defenceless her draught prevented her escape. By the orders of her captain she was therefore burned and sunk. The joy which her exploit had evoked throughout the Confederacy now turned to grief and anger. But the Confederate court-martial upon the captain declared that "The only alternative, in the opinion of the court, was to abandon and burn the ship then and there; which in the judgment of the court was deliberately and wisely done by order of the accused."

CHAPTER FIVE

Lee and McClellan

G ENERAL POPE reached the front on August 1, 1862. The new commander's task was plainly to gain as much ground as he could without being seriously engaged until McClellan's army could return from the James River and join him. Aquia Creek, not far south of the capital, was appointed for the landing of this army, and further large reinforcements were moving from Washington, through Alexandria, and along the railroad. Pope had already forty thousand men; in six weeks he would have a hundred and fifty thousand. He was full of energy, and very sanguine. He hoped to capture both Gordonsville and Charlottesville even before his main force arrived, and then finish off Richmond.

As soon as Lee saw that McClellan had no further bite he sent Jackson, in the middle of July, with two divisions (eleven thousand men) to Gordonsville, and raised him by the end of the month to twenty-four thousand. This was a lot for Jackson, who had barely two to one to face. He found Pope's army moving hopefully towards him by the three roads which joined at Culpeper. On August 9 he fell upon General Banks, commanding Pope's leading corps, seven miles south of Culpeper, at Cedar Mountain. He used twenty thousand men against Banks's nine thousand, drove them from the field with the loss of a quarter of their number, and left the rest in no condition to do more than guard the baggage. But before Culpeper he found himself confronted with the other two corps of Pope's army, and in harmony with Lee's conceptions he fell back to Gordonsville.

On August 13 Lee learnt that McClellan's army was being re-embarked at Fortress Monroe. This was the signal for which he was waiting. Before this splendid army could make its weight tell with Pope in Northern Virginia, a period of a month at the outside, he must win a great battle there. He at once ordered General James Longstreet with twelve brigades, the bulk of the Richmond forces, to join Jackson at Gordonsville, and by the 17th he had fifty-five thousand men concentrated in the woods behind Clark's Mountain, within striking distance of Culpeper, where Pope was now established. Pope was unaware of his peril, and might well have been destroyed. But Lee waited a day to bring up his cavalry, and in the meantime a Confederate officer was captured with papers which opened Pope's eyes. Favoured by the morning mist, he retreated forthwith behind the Rappahannock. Lee's first right-handed clutch had failed. He now scooped with the left hand. Jackson crossed the Upper Rappahannock by Sulphur Springs. But the river rose after his first brigade was over, and a second time Pope was saved.

Lee now knew that his brief period of superiority had passed, and that he must expect, in a week or ten days, overwhelming forces to be massed against him. He knew that the leading divisions of McClellan's former army were already ashore at Aquia Creek. How could the Army of Northern Virginia cope with a hundred and fifty thousand men, once they were concentrated? He therefore resolved with Jackson upon a daring and, since it was successful, brilliant manœuvre. In the face of a superior and rapidly growing enemy he divided his army. Before dawn on August 25 Jackson began another of his famous marches. With twenty thousand men, after covering twenty-six miles, he reached Salem, far behind Pope's right flank, and the next day by another twenty-five-mile march through Thoroughfare Gap in the hills he cut the Alexandria-Orange railway, upon which Pope depended for his supplies, a few miles south of Manassas Junction. On the 27th he seized the junction. Here the whole supply of Pope's army was heaped. Food, equipment, stores of every kind, dazzling to the pinched Confederates, fell into his hands. He set guards upon the liquor and let his men take what they could carry. Most of them reclothed themselves. But this booty might be bought at a fatal price. On every side superior Federal forces lay or were approaching. The cutting of Pope's communications was an incident and not the aim of Jackson and his chief. Nothing short of a great battle won was of any use to them. He therefore delivered the junction and its depot to the flames. Looking northwards, Pope perceived the night sky reddened by the immense conflagration. It was Jackson's part to keep him puzzled and occupied till Lee could come round with Longstreet and the main army and join him.

There was now no danger of Pope marching on towards Richmond. He was hamstrung. He must retreat. But with the great forces arriving by every road to join him he would still have a large preponderance. He might even close Thoroughfare Gap to Lee and the rest of the Confederate Army. It was a dire hazard of war. Jackson withdrew from Manassas Junction northward into the woods by Sudley Springs. Pope, believing that he had him in his grip at the Junction, marched upon it from every quarter. The Junction was found in ashes and empty. During the 28th neither side knew all that was happening; but Jackson was aware that Longstreet was thrusting through Thoroughfare Gap with Lee and the main Confederate Army. Pope's orders to his disjointed army were to annihilate Jackson, now located south of Sudley Springs,

THE BATTLEFIELDS OF VIRGINIA

Confederate earthworks for the defences of Richmond ⋀⋀⋀

0 ——— 10 ——— 20
Miles

Urbana

Pamunkey R.

Ashland

Mechanicsville
Gaines's Mill
Cold Harbour
Fair Oaks
Savages Station
Seven Pines
Chickahominy R.
White Oak Swamp
Frayser's Farm
Malvern Hill
Harrison's Landing

Richmond
James R.
James R.

Petersburg
Appomattox R.

and for this purpose he set seventy thousand men in motion. He thought only of Jackson. He seemed to have forgotten Longstreet and Lee, who were already massing into line on Jackson's right.

On August 30 began the Second Battle of Bull Run, or Manassas. With great bravery fifty-three thousand Federals in five successive assaults grappled in the open field with Jackson's twenty thousand. To and fro the struggle swayed, with equal slaughter. Longstreet, already in line, but still unperceived, was painfully slow in coming into action. He always wished to look before he leapt; and this sound maxim was far below the level of the event. He was a great war-horse, and Lee would not press him beyond a certain point. On the first day of the Second Manassas Jackson bore the whole brunt alone. As evening came, when his last reserves had delivered their counter-attack, a clergyman with whom he was friendly expressed his fears for the thin-worn Confederate left. "Stonewall," measuring the struggle from minute to minute, took one long look at the field and said, "They have done their worst."

Battle was renewed at dawn on the 31st. Pope had received the support of two new corps, marching up from Aquia. Still unconscious of Longstreet's presence, he ordered the ill-starred General, Porter, to turn Jackson's right, and Porter's troops responded loyally. But now Longstreet, massive once he was in action, threw in the main weight of the Confederate Army. Pope's array was ruptured. On a four-mile front the new, unexpected Confederate Army debouched magnificently from the woods. The two corps of Pope's left, outnumbered and outflanked, retreated. Porter, enveloped, was overwhelmed, and subsequently victimised by court-martial. Although even at the end of the day Pope commanded 70,000 faithful men, he had no thought but to seek shelter behind the Washington entrenchments, into which he also carried with him a final reinforcement of 10,000 men which reached him during the night. Lee had captured thirty guns, 20,000 precious rifles, and 7,000 prisoners, and had killed and wounded 13,500 Federals, at a total cost to the Confederacy of 10,000 men. He had utterly defeated 75,000 Union troops with less than 55,000 in his own hand. It was exactly four months since President Davis had given him command. Then McClellan was within five miles of Richmond. Now Lee's outposts were within twenty miles of Washington. In this decisive manner the tables were turned.

*   *   *   *   *

Ill-treatment was meted out to General McClellan by the Washington politicians and Cabinet, with the cautious, pliant General Halleck as their tool. For this Lincoln cannot escape blame. He wanted an aggressive General who would energetically seek out Lee and beat him. McClellan for all his qualities of leadership lacked the final ounces of fighting spirit. Lincoln with his shrewd judgment of men knew this. But he also knew that McClellan was probably the ablest commander available to him. His instinct had been to stand by his chosen General. Instead he had yielded to political outcry. He had swapped horses in mid-stream. He found he had got a poorer mount. As the different corps of McClellan's army were landed at Aquia they were hurried off to join Pope, until McClellan had not even his own personal escort with him. Yet he was never removed from the command of the Army of Virginia, which had been renamed the Army of the Potomac. He made voluble and justified complaints, to which no attention was paid. But on September 2, when Pope and his beaten army seemed about to collapse upon Washington, and panic lapped around the President, a different attitude was shown. While McClellan was breakfasting that morning he was visited by the President and the General-in-Chief. Halleck declared that Washington was lost, and offered McClellan the command of all the forces. The flouted commander at once undertook to save the city. As he had never been dismissed officially, he was never reappointed. He had been deprived of all his troops; they were now restored. History has never allowed McClellan to rise above the level of competent and courageous mediocrity; but it must not be forgotten that when he rode out to meet the retreating army they received him with frantic enthusiasm. The long, jaded, humiliated columns of brave men who had been so shamefully mishandled broke their ranks and almost dragged their restored commander from the saddle. The soldiers embraced and kissed his horse's legs. Thus fortified, McClellan restored order to the army and turned its face again to the foe.

Lee, after the second Confederate victory at Manassas, did what ought to have been done after the first. He invaded Maryland to give that state a chance to come over, if it still would or could. Always seeking the decisive and final battle which he knew could alone save the Confederacy, he marched north by Leesburg, crossed the Potomac, and arrived in the neighbourhood of Frederick, abreast of Baltimore. He knew he had never the slightest chance of taking Washington; but there were prizes to be won in the open field. Three Federal garrisons occupied Martinsburg, Winchester, and Harpers Ferry, in the Shenandoah valley. At Harpers Ferry there was a great Union depot of supply. In the three places there were over fifteen thousand men. Halleck had refused to withdraw them while time remained. They became a substantial objective to Lee, and his design was to capture Harpers Ferry, into which the two smaller garrisons withdrew. Accordingly he marched west from Frederick through the range of hills called the South Mountains, sent Jackson looping out by Martinsburg, and on September 13 closed down on Harpers Ferry from all sides.

The Washington politicians, in their hour of panic, had clung to McClellan. They did not mean to sink with him. He was originally given orders only to defend the Washington fortifications. However, on his own responsibility, or, so he later claimed, "with a rope round his neck," he took charge of his old army, quitted "the Washington defences," and set out after Lee, whom he outnumbered by two to one. McClellan's account of this episode is widely contested, for in fact Lincoln discussed with him the Army's movement into Maryland and verbally gave him "command of the forces in the field" as well as around the capital. McClellan's political prejudices may well have coloured his memory. He had reason to feel aggrieved. His innumerable critics in high places never ceased to harry him. Their attitude to the commander in the field at this juncture was dishonouring to them.

McClellan, hoping to save Harpers Ferry, now started after Lee with nearly ninety thousand men, including two fine corps that had not yet suffered at all. By a stroke of luck a Northern private soldier picked up three cigars wrapped in a piece of paper which was in fact a copy of Lee's most secret orders. McClellan learned on the 13th that Lee had divided his army and that the bulk of it was closing on Harpers Ferry. He therefore advanced with very good assurance to attack him. Everything now became a matter of hours. Could Jackson, Walner, and McLaws capture Harpers Ferry before Lee was beaten in the passes of the South Mountains?

McClellan wasted many of these precious hours. But considering that members of the Government behind him could only gape and gibber and that his political foes were avid of a chance to bring him to ruin it is not surprising that he acted with a double dose of his habitual caution. By overwhelming forces Lee was beaten back from the two gaps in the South Mountain range on the 14th. He now had to take a great decision. At first he thought to gather his spoils and laurels and re-cross the Potomac into Virginia. But later, feeling that nothing but victory would suffice, he resolved to give battle behind the Antietam stream, with his back to the Potomac, believing that Jackson would capture Harpers Ferry in the meanwhile and rejoin him in time.

Harpers Ferry surrendered early on the 15th. Seventy-three guns, thirteen thousand rifles, and twelve thousand five hundred prisoners were gathered by Jackson's officers. He was himself already marching all through the afternoon and night to join Lee, who stood with but twenty thousand men against the vast approaching mass of McClellan. This worthy general was unable to free himself from the Washington obsession. Had he been as great a soldier or as great a man as Lee he would have staked all on the battle. But he could not free his mind from the cowardly and personally malignant political forces behind him. To make sure of not running undue risks, he lost a day, and failed to win the battle.

It was not till the 17th that he attacked. By this time Jackson had arrived and was posted on Lee's left, and the rest of the Confederate divisions, having cleaned up Harpers Ferry, were striding along to the new encounter. Lee fought with his back to the Potomac, and could scarcely, if defeated, have escaped across its single bridge by Sharpsburg. This horrible battle was the acme of Federal mismanagement. McClellan, after riding down the line, fought it from his headquarters on what was called "the Commander-in-Chief idea." This meant that he made his dispositions and left the battle to fight itself. But Jackson stood in the line, and Lee rode his horse about the field controlling the storm, as Marlborough, Frederick the Great, and Napoleon were wont to do. The Confederate left,

THE BATTLE OF CHICKAMAUGA

Lee and Gordon's Mills, on the bank of the Chickamauga, between
Missionary Ridge and Pigeon Mountain

GENERAL ULYSSES S. GRANT
Appointed Commander-in-Chief of the United States Army on March 9, 1864

"THE SAVAGE COUNTRY OF THE WILDERNESS"
The field of the bloody battles of May 5 and 6, 1864

TEN MINUTES WITH GRANT AND HIS STAFF

The scene at the staff conference on June 2, 1864, the day before the battle of Cold Harbour. In the first photograph (*top left*) Grant sits with his back to the tree on the left. On Grant's right is General Porter, on his left his chief-of-staff, General Rawlins. Colonel Bowers, his adjutant-general, is standing, reading a report, on the right of the picture. In the second photograph (*bottom left*) Grant has moved to the back of the bench, left, and is leaning over the shoulder of General Meade, consulting a map. In the final photograph (*above*) the Commander-in-Chief is back in his seat, composing his orders for the following day.

THE DEFENCES BEFORE ATLANTA

The palisades earthworks constructed by General Joseph F. Johnston before he was superseded by General John B. Hood. Atlanta fell to Sherman after a prolonged siege.

ANDERSONVILLE

The notorious Confederate prison-camp in Georgia. These two photographs, taken in August 1864, show (*above*) the appalling conditions of the camp, with shelters erected right up to the "Dead Line," which prisoners crossed only at the risk of being shot, and (*below*) an issue of the meagre rations.

THE LAST TRAIN FROM ATLANTA

The result of Sherman's eviction order of September 1864. "I propose to use it purely for our own military purposes which are inconsistent with its habitation by the families of a brave people. I am shipping them *all*. . . ."

under Jackson, was practically destroyed, but only after ruining double their numbers, two whole corps of the Federal Army. All here came to a standstill, till Jackson was reinforced by Lee from his hard-pressed right and centre. The Union centre then attacked piecemeal, and their leading division was torn to pieces, half falling smitten. Burnside, who with the Union left was to cross the Antietam and cut Lee's line of retreat, would have succeeded but for the arrival of Lee's last division, under A. P. Hill, from Harpers Ferry. Striking the right flank of the assailants from an unexpected direction, he ended this menace; and night fell upon a drawn battle, in which the Federals had lost thirteen thousand men, a fourth of the troops they engaged and one-sixth of those they had on the field, and the Confederacy nine thousand, which was about a quarter.

When darkness fell Lee faced his great lieutenants. Without exception they advised immediate retreat across the Potomac. Even Jackson, unconquerable in action, thought this would be wise. But Lee, who still hoped to gain his indisputable, decisive battle, after hearing all opinions, declared his resolve to stand his ground. Therefore the shattered Confederates faced the morning light and the huge array of valiant soldiers who seemed about to overwhelm them. But McClellan had had enough. He lay still. Before the slightest reproach can fall on him the shabby War Department behind him must shoulder their share. There was no fighting on the 18th. Lee put it hard across Jackson to take the offensive; but when Jackson, after personal reconnaissance with the artillery commander, declared it impossible Lee accepted this sagacious judgment, and his first invasion of Maryland came to an end.

War had never reached such an intensity of moral and physical forces focused upon decisive points as in this campaign of 1862. The number of battles that were fought and their desperate, bloody character far surpassed any events in which Napoleon ever moved. From June 1, when Lee was given the command, the Army of Northern Virginia fought seven ferocious battles—the Seven Days, Cedar Run, the Second Manassas, South Mountain, Harpers Ferry, the Antietam, and later Fredericksburg—in as many months. Lee very rarely had three-quarters, and several times only half, the strength of his opponents. These brave Northerners were certainly hampered by a woeful political direction, but, on the other side, the Confederates were short of weapons, ammunition, food, equipment, clothes, and boots. It was even said that their line of march could be traced by the bloodstained footprints of unshod men. But the Army of Northern Virginia "carried the Confederacy on its bayonets" and made a struggle unsurpassed in history.

* * * * *

Lincoln had hoped for a signal victory. McClellan at the Antietam presented him with a partial though important success. But the President's faith in the Union cause was never dimmed by disappointments. He was much beset by anxieties, which led him to cross-examine his commanders as if he were still a prosecuting attorney. The Generals did not relish it. But Lincoln's popularity with the troops stood high. They put their trust in him. They could have no knowledge of the relentless political pressures in Washington to which he was subjected. They had a sense however of his natural resolution and generosity of character. He had to draw deeply on these qualities in his work at the White House. Through his office flowed a stream of politicians, newspaper editors, and other men of influence. Most of them clamoured for quick victory, with no conception of the hazards of war. Many of them cherished their own amateur plans of operation which they confidently urged upon their leader. Many of them too had favourite Generals for whom they canvassed. Lincoln treated all his visitors with patience and firmness. His homely humour stood him in good stead. A sense of irony helped to lighten his burdens. In tense moments a dry joke relieved his feelings. At the same time his spirit was sustained by a deepening belief in Providence. When the toll of war rose steeply and plans went wrong he appealed for strength in his inmost thoughts to a power higher than man's. Strength was certainly given him. It is sometimes necessary at the summit of authority to bear with the intrigues of disloyal colleagues, to remain calm when others panic, and to withstand misguided popular outcries. All this Lincoln did. Personal troubles also befell him. One of his beloved sons died in the White House. Mrs Lincoln, though devoted to her husband, had a taste for extravagance and for politics which sometimes gave rise to wounding comment. As the war drew on Lincoln became more and more gaunt and the furrows on his cheeks and brow bit deep. Fortitude was written on his countenance.

The Antietam and the withdrawal of Lee into Virginia gave the President an opportunity to take a momentous step. He proclaimed the emancipation of all the slaves in the insurgent states. The impression produced in France and Britain by Lee's spirited and resolute operations, with their successive great battles, either victorious or drawn, made the Washington Cabinet fearful of mediation, to be followed, if rejected, by recognition of the Confederacy. The North was discouraged by disastrous and futile losses and by the sense of being out-generalled. Recruitment fell off and desertion was rife. Many urged peace, and others asked whether the Union was worthy of this slaughter, if slavery was to be maintained. By casting down this final challenge and raising the war to the level of a moral crusade Lincoln hoped to rally British public opinion to the Union cause and raise a new enthusiasm among his own fellow-countrymen.

It was a move he had long considered. Even since the beginning of the war the Radicals had been pressing for the total abolition of slavery. Lincoln had misgivings about the effects on the slave-owning states of the border which had remained loyal. He insisted that the sole object of the war was to preserve the Union. As he wrote to the New York publisher, Horace Greeley, "My paramount object is to save the Union, and is not either to save or to destroy slavery. . . . What I do about slavery and the coloured race, I do because it helps to save the Union; and what I forbear, I forbear because I do not believe it would help to save the Union." Meanwhile he was meditating on the timing of his Proclamation and on the constitutional difficulties that stood in the way. He believed he had no power to interfere with slavery in the border states. He felt his Proclamation could be legally justified only as a military measure, issued in virtue of his office as Commander-in-Chief of the Army and Navy. Its intention was to deprive the Confederacy of a source of its strength. When the Proclamation was published, with effect from January 1st, 1863, it therefore applied only to the rebel states. Slavery in the rest of the Union was not finally abolished until the passing of the Thirteenth Amendment in December 1865. In the South the Proclamation only came into force as the Federal armies advanced. Nor were the broader results all that Lincoln had hoped. In Britain it was not understood why he had not declared Abolition outright. A political manœuvre on his part was suspected. In America itself the war assumed an implacable character, offering to the South no alternative but subjugation. The Democratic Party in the North was wholly opposed to the Emancipation Edict. In the Federal armies it was unpopular, and General

McClellan, who might be expected to become the Democratic candidate for the Presidency, had two months earlier sent Lincoln a solemn warning against such an action. At the Congressional elections in the autumn of 1862 the Republicans lost ground. Many Northerners thought that the President had gone too far, others that he had not gone far enough. Great, judicious, and well-considered steps are thus sometimes at first received with public incomprehension.

The relations between the Washington Government and its General remained deplorable. McClellan might fairly claim to have rendered them an immense service after the panic at Manassas. He had revived the Army, led it to the field, and cleared Maryland. For all the Government knew, he had saved the capital. In fact he had done more. Lord Palmerston in England had decided that summer on mediation. News of the Antietam made him hesitate. This averted the danger to the North that the Confederacy would be recognised by the Powers of Europe. But it was not immediately apparent in the Union. Gladstone, Chancellor of the Exchequer in Palmerston's Government, delivered a speech at Newcastle in the autumn which enraged Northern opinion. He said: "We know quite well that the people of the Northern states have not yet drunk of the cup—they are still trying to hold it from their lips—which all the world sees they nevertheless must drink of. We may have our own opinions about slavery, we may be for or against the South, but there is no doubt that Jefferson Davis and other leaders of the South have made an Army; they are making, it appears, a Navy; and they have made what is more than either, they have made a Nation." Gladstone had not been informed that Palmerston had changed his mind.

Meanwhile between the politicians and the Commander-in-Chief upon the Potomac there was hatred and scorn on both sides. Bitter party politics aggravated military divergence. The President desired a prompt and vigorous advance. McClellan, as usual, magnified Confederate numbers and underrated their grievous losses. He was determined to run no unmilitary risks for a Government which he knew was eager to stab him in the back. Five weeks passed after the battle before he began to cross the Potomac in leisurely fashion and move forward from Harpers Ferry to Warrenton.

Lee withdrew by easy marches up the Shenandoah valley. He had sent "Jeb" Stuart on his second romantic ride round McClellan in mid-October, had harried the Federal communications and acquired much valuable information. He now did not hesitate to divide his army in the face of McClellan's great hosts. He left Jackson in the valley to keep Washington on tenterhooks, and rested himself with Longstreet, near Culpeper Court House. If pressed he could fall back to Gordonsville, where he judged Jackson could join him in time. McClellan however had now at length prepared his blow. He planned to strike Lee with overwhelming strength before Jackson could return. At this moment he was himself taken in rear by President Lincoln. On the night of November 7, 1862, he was ordered to hand over his command to General Burnside, and at the same time Porter, his most competent subordinate, was placed under arrest. The Government had used these men in their desperation. They now felt strong enough to strike them down. McClellan was against the abolition of slavery, and he never changed his view. The dominant Radical wing of the Republican Party was out for his blood. They were convinced that McClellan would never set himself to gain a crushing victory. They suspected him of tender feelings for the South and a desire for a negotiated peace. They also feared that the General would prove to be a potent Democratic candidate for the Presidency. Lincoln allowed himself to be persuaded by the Radical Republicans that McClellan had become a liability to his Government. He had long stood up for his commander against the attacks and whisperings of the politicians. Now he felt he must give way. But it was without animosity, for that viper was never harboured in Lincoln's breast.

There was almost a mutiny in the Union Army when McClellan's dismissal was known. He himself acted with perfect propriety, and used all his influence to place his successor in the saddle. He was never employed again. Thus the General who, as Lee after the war told his youngest son, was by far the best of his opponents disappeared from command. No one can be blind to McClellan's limitations, but he was learning continually from his collisions with Lee and Jackson. His removal was a wrong done to the Union Army, which never gave its love to any other leader. There remained for McClellan a vivid political struggle where numbers, which alone count in such affairs, were found upon the other side. General Porter, although he had rendered good service in the intervening Maryland campaign, was tried by court-martial for his conduct at the Second Manassas, condemned, and dismissed from the United States Army. This injustice was repaired after the lapse of years. A re-trial was ordered and he received honourable acquittal.

We have seen several times in this obstinate war President Lincoln pressing for battle and for frontal attack. "On to Richmond" was his mood; and now at last in Burnside he had found a General who would butt straight at the barrier. Burnside, a charming personality, but a thoroughly bad General, was, to his honour, most reluctant to take command. Once in charge he followed a simple plan. He chose the shortest road which led on the map to Richmond, and concentrated his army along it upon the crossing of the Rappahannock at Fredericksburg.

He took a fortnight in order to do this as well as possible.

Meanwhile Lee brought in Jackson and other reinforcements. Hitherto Lee had always fought in the open field; even against the heavy odds of the Antietam he had not used the spade. He now applied the fortnight accorded him to fortify his position above Fredericksburg with every then-known device. Breastworks revetted with logs and stone walls covered by solid earth were prepared. Nearly a hundred and fifty cannon were comfortably sited. Rifle-pits abounded, and good lateral roads were cut through the scrubby forest behind the line. On December 11 Burnside occupied Fredericksburg, crossed the river with a large part of his army, and deployed for battle. He had a hundred and eighteen thousand men, against Lee's eighty thousand. On the 13th he delivered his assault. He attacked both the Confederate left wing and its right piecemeal. Then he attacked in the centre. The Northern soldiers showed an intense devotion. Brigade after brigade, division after division, they charged up the slopes under a murderous fire. As evening fell the Union army recoiled with a loss of nearly thirteen thousand men. The Confederate casualties, mostly in Jackson's command, were under six thousand. Burnside, who now thought chiefly of dying at the head of his troops, wished to renew the battle next day. He was restrained by universal opinion at the front and at the capital; and soon after was superseded in chief command by one of his lieutenants, General Joseph Hooker.

Lee had not wished to fight at Fredericksburg at all. The Federal Army was so near its salt-water base at Aquia Creek that no counter-stroke was possible. He had advised President Davis to let him meet Burnside thirty miles back on the North Anna River, where there was room for him to use Jackson and Stuart in terrible revenge upon the communications of a repulsed army. But although Davis' relations with the Confederate Generals were on a high plane he had hampered his champion most sadly, cramping him down to a strict defensive, and thus the shattering blow of Fredericksburg had no lasting consequences. If these two Presidents had let McClellan and Lee fight the quarrel out between them as they thought best the end would have been the same, but the war would have been less muddled, much shorter, and less bloody.

* * * * *

In the West nothing decisive had happened up till the end of 1862. By November General Joseph E. Johnston, having recovered from the wounds he got at Seven Pines, was appointed to the chief Confederate command in this theatre, but with only a partial authority over its various armies. In Tennessee General Bragg, with forty-four thousand men in the neighbourhood of Murfreesboro, faced the Federal General William S. Rosecrans, who had forty-seven thousand. General J. C. Pemberton, who commanded the department of the Mississippi, had a field army of about thirty thousand men, apart from the garrisons of Vicksburg and Port Hudson. Lastly, still farther west, in Arkansas, the Confederate General Holmes was encamped near Little Rock with an army raised in that state of fifty thousand men, against whom there were now no active Federal forces. When it was evident that Grant was preparing for the invasion of Mississippi and an attack upon Vicksburg Johnston urged that the Arkansas army should cross the Mississippi and join Pemberton. This would have secured a Confederate superiority. Jefferson Davis vetoed this desirable, and indeed imperative, measure. He knew the violent hostility which an order to the Arkansas forces to serve east of the Mississippi would excite throughout the Western states. No doubt this objection was substantial; but the alternative was disastrous. The President insisted instead that Bragg should send ten thousand men from Chattanooga to strengthen Pemberton in defending Vicksburg. This was accordingly done.

Early in December Grant made a renewed attempt against Vicksburg, sending General Sherman from Memphis, with about thirty thousand men, and Admiral Porter's Naval Squadron, to enter the Yazoo River and occupy the heights to the north of the city. Sherman assaulted the Confederate defences at Chickasaw Bluff on December 29, and in less than an hour was repulsed with the loss of nearly two thousand men, the Confederates losing only a hundred and fifty. He consoled himself with ascending the Arkansas River and capturing a garrison of five thousand Confederates at Arkansas Post. Meanwhile the weakening of Bragg's army in Tennessee brought about, on the last day of the year, a severe battle at Murfreesboro, in which the greatest bravery was displayed by both sides. The Federals, under Rosecrans, lost over nine thousand killed and wounded, as well as nearly four thousand prisoners and twenty-eight guns. But for this Bragg paid over ten thousand men. The Federal hold on Tennessee and its capital Nashville was unshaken. Bragg withdrew his disappointed troops into winter quarters covering Chattanooga.

The armies in the different states still confronted each other on fairly equal terms, and although the Union Navy declared its ability to run the gauntlet of the Confederate batteries when required the great riverway remained barred to Federal transports and traffic. Murfreesboro gave the impression of a drawn battle, and Chickasaw Bluff was an undoubted Confederate success. But now there was to be a profound change in the balance.

CHAPTER SIX

Chancellorsville and Gettysburg

THE spring of 1863 found the Army of the Potomac and the Army of Northern Virginia still facing each other across the Rappahannock. Hooker, "Fighting Joe," had distinguished himself as a corps commander at the Antietam. He was not the next senior and had intrigued against his chief. He owed his present advancement to Lincoln, who knew him to be a good fighter and hoped the best of him as a commander. The obvious course, to restore McClellan again, was politically impossible and would have weakened the President's authority. At the end of January, when he was appointed, Hooker found the Federal Army in a sorry plight, which his own previous discontent had fomented. More than three thousand officers and eighty thousand men were either deserters or absent with or without leave. Blows like Fredericksburg are hard to sustain. It was not till April that reorganisation was complete; reinforcements had poured in, and the absentees had returned from their Christmas at home. He was now at the head of over a hundred and thirty thousand men, rested and revived, splendidly equipped, and organised in six army corps. He formed besides a cavalry corps ten thousand strong, and he felt himself able to declare that he led "the finest army on the planet."

In meeting the offensive, which he knew must come, Lee

was gravely hampered by President Davis's policy of the strict defensive and the dispersal of the Confederate troops to cover a number of places. The continued pressure of the war rendered the defence of the ports of Wilmington and Charleston in South Carolina of vital importance, though only blockade-runners could enter them. They and the railways connecting them with Richmond were threatened in the President's eyes by the somewhat near presence of Federal forces which had been landed in March 1862 at New Bern, in North Carolina, and others which had advanced to Suffolk in the estuary of the James River and only seventy-five miles from Richmond. These parties, owing to the nature of the ground near the coast, had been dealt with by local forces. But Lee, also bearing in mind the difficulty of feeding his troops near the Rappahannock, sent first one, then a second and a third detachment, under Longstreet, to deal with them. It was one of Lee's mistakes. Longstreet, who was always striving for an independent command, unnecessarily sat down to besiege Suffolk. Thus Lee's nine divisions were reduced by three, and two of his four cavalry brigades were south of the James to gather forage. His infantry was less than half and his cavalry a quarter of the forces he had to encounter. He therefore abandoned the idea of an offensive into Pennsylvania by way of the Shenandoah valley, which he had had in mind, and awaited events.

Hooker's preponderance enabled him to act with two armies. His plan was, first, a fortnight in advance of the main move, to send his cavalry round Lee's left by the upper fords of the Rappahannock; then to turn Lee's left with three corps, while the two others, under General John Sedgwick, crossed the river below Lee's right at Fredericksburg. Even then he had another corps in reserve. He expected that Lee would be forced to abandon his lines and retreat, in which case he meant to follow him up by the direct road to Richmond. In the middle of April these movements began. The Federal cavalry corps, under a second-rate commander, General George Stoneman, was delayed by floods, and only crossed the Upper Rappahannock simultaneously with the right column of the main army.

At first all went well with Hooker. His three army corps, about seventy thousand strong, crossed the Rappahannock, and, on the morning of April 30, its tributary the Rapidan. As they marched eastward they took in flank and rear the fortified line which Lee had formed. The Confederates guarding United States Ford on the Rappahannock had to retire, and the reserve Federal corps passed over unmolested. By the night of the 30th a Federal army of ninety thousand men was concentrated at or near Chancellorsville behind all these defences. The Federal cavalry, in enormous, though not as it proved overwhelming strength, were already moving towards the Virginia Central Railway, forty-five miles in rear of Lee's army, and one of his main lines of supply, which it was their mission not only to cut but to destroy. At the same time General Sedgwick, commanding the two corps opposite Fredericksburg, crossed the river and deployed to attack Jackson's three divisions under General Jubal A. Early, which held the old trenches of the former battle.

Lee was thus taken in pincers by two armies, each capable of fighting a major battle with him, while at the same time his rear was ravaged and his communications assailed. The advance of either Federal Army would render his position untenable, and their junction or simultaneous action in a single battle must destroy him. Nothing more hopeless on the map than his position on the night of the 30th can be imagined, and it is this which raises the event which followed from a military to an historic level.

The great commander and his trusty lieutenant remained crouched but confident amid this tremendous encirclement. Beset upon both flanks by hostile armies which were for the moment disconnected, and unable to retreat without yielding vital positions, Lee naturally sought to hold off one assailant while striking at the other. Which to choose? Jackson was for falling upon Sedgwick and driving him into the river; but Lee knew that nothing less than the defeat of the main Union army would save him. Hooker had taken command in person of this mighty array, and Lee, as soon as he learned where he was, left only a division to delay Sedgwick and marched at once to attack him. Meanwhile "Jeb" Stuart manœuvred against Stoneman's cavalry over a wide front to such good purpose that though he was outnumbered by four to one he was able to render perfect service to Lee, while the Federal cavalry General, Stoneman, played no part in the battle.

* * * * *

Chancellorsville stands on the edge of a wild region of forest and tangled scrub which still deserves the name of Wilderness. Roads or paths cut through this alone rendered movement possible. On May 1 Hooker, having brought up all his troops, ordered a general advance eastward along the Turnpike and the Plank road. His numerous cavalry were breaking up the Virginia Central Railway at Louisa Court House, thirty miles to the southward. He had three balloons and numerous signal stations, and even a field electric telegraph for communication with Sedgwick. But the mist of the morning lay in fog-banks over the valley of the Rappahannock. The balloons and signal stations could see nothing, and the electric telegraph broke down. As he advanced into the Wilderness he met large enemy forces, who began at once to attack him. These were Stonewall Jackson's corps, handled with its general's usual vigour. Now "Fighting Joe," so famous as a subordinate, bent under the strain of supreme command. He had expected that his well-executed strategy would compel Lee to retreat. He now conceived himself about to be attacked by the whole Confederate Army. He turned at once and fell back upon the entrenched line he had already prudently prepared before Chancellorsville. It was late in the afternoon of the 1st when the advancing Confederates, emerging from the woodland, came within sight of this formidable position with its masses of troops. All the time Sedgwick, at Fredericksburg, receiving no orders by the electric telegraph, and, baffled by Early's brave show on the fatal heights, already dyed with Union blood, although he heard the firing, made no effort. How did he know that Longstreet might not have arrived, as would indeed have been only proper? Thus the night set in.

Lee and Jackson sat together, and knew that they had one day before them. Unless they could beat Hooker at odds of two to one during May 2 they would be attacked front and rear by overwhelming forces. Frontal attack was impossible. Their only chance was to divide their small army and swing round Hooker's right. Search had been made for a road or track for such a movement; and in the small hours one of Jackson's staff officers reported that there was a private road used for hauling wood and ore to a furnace which would serve. Jackson at once proposed to lead his whole corps along it, and Lee after a moment's reflection assented. This meant that Jackson with twenty-six thousand men would march round Hooker's right to attack him, while Lee faced nearly eighty thousand Federals with seventeen thousand.

At 4 A.M. Jackson was on the march. It seemed vital that his movement should be unperceived, but an unexpected gap in the forest revealed about eight o'clock to the Federal troops at Hazel Grove a long column moving towards the right of their wide front. This exposure actually helped the Confederate manœuvre. Two divisions of General Daniel E. Sickles's corps advanced after some delay to strike at these processionists and find out their purpose. They came into contact with Jackson's rearguard, who fought stubbornly, and then vanished in the woods. The two divisions, now joined by Sickles himself, feeling they had a retreating enemy before them, pushed on hopefully, and Sickles thought he had cut the Confederate Army in twain. This was indeed true. Lee and Jackson were now separated, and only victory could reunite them. Had Hooker set his army in motion against Lee he must have driven Lee ever farther from Jackson and ever nearer to Sedgwick, who had now at length forced the heights of Fredericksburg, and, little more than eight miles away, was, with thirty thousand men, driving Early back upon Lee's rear. But Hooker, convinced that he was safe within his fortifications and that his strategy was successful, made no move, while the hours slipped away. It was six o'clock in the evening before Jackson reached the end of his march. He had not only turned Hooker's flank, but was actually in rear of his right-hand corps. He deployed into line, facing Lee about four miles away on the other side of the Federal Army. The surprise was complete. The soldiers of the Eleventh Federal Corps were eating their supper and playing cards behind their defences when suddenly there burst from the forest at their backs the Confederate line of battle. In one hour the Eleventh Corps, attacked by superior forces in this battle, although as a whole their army was two to one, was dashed into rout and ruin.

Night was falling, but Jackson saw supreme opportunity before him. He was within half a mile of the road leading to

United States Ford, the sole line of retreat for Hooker's whole army, and between him and this deadly thrust no organised force intervened. He selected the point which he must gain by night and hold to the death at dawn. The prize was nothing less than the destruction of the main Federal Army. They must either overwhelm him the next day or starve between the Wilderness and his cannon. All this he saw. He rode forward with a handful of officers along the Plank road to the skirmish line to see what he could of the ground. He had often risked his life in this way, and now the forfeit was claimed. As he returned, his own men, Carolinians proud to die at his command, mistaking in the darkness the small party for hostile cavalry, fired a volley. Three bullets pierced the General's left arm and shoulder. He fell from his horse, and when, after an agonising passage, he reached the field hospital he was too much weakened by loss of blood to concentrate his mind. His staff officer, who was to lead A. P. Hill's division to the vital point, had been killed by the same volley. Hill, on whom the command devolved, hastening forward after vainly questioning his swooning chief, was almost immediately himself wounded. It was some hours before Stuart, from the cavalry, could be brought to the scene. No one knew Jackson's plan, and he was now unconscious. Thus on small agate points do the balances of the world turn.

Stuart fought a fine battle during the night, and on May 3, with wild shouts of "Remember Jackson!" the infuriated Confederates assaulted the Federal line. They drove it back. They captured Hazel Grove. They joined hands again with Lee. But the chance of the night was gone for ever. Hooker now had masses of men covering his line of retreat to the ford. He now thought of nothing but retreat. He did not even keep Lee occupied upon his front. He was morally beaten on the 2nd, and during the battle of the 3rd a solid shot hitting the pillar of a house by which he stood stunned him, which was perhaps a merciful stroke.

Lee now turned on Sedgwick, whose position south of the river was one of great peril. He had fought hard during the whole of the 3rd, and found himself on the 4th with the river at his back and only twenty thousand effective men, attacked by Lee, with at least twenty-five thousand. But the Confederate soldiers were exhausted by their superhuman exertions. Sedgwick, though beaten and mauled, managed to escape by his pontoons at Fredericksburg. Here he was soon joined by the Commander-in-Chief and the rest of the magnificent army which nine days before had seemed to have certain success in their path, but now stood baffled and humbled at their starting-point. They were still twice as numerous as their opponents. They had lost 17,000 men out of 130,000 and the Confederates 12,500 out of 60,000.

Chancellorsville was the finest battle which Lee and Jackson fought together. Their combination had become perfect. "Such an executive officer," said Lee, "the sun never shone on. Straight as the needle to the pole, he advances to the execution of my purpose." "I would follow General Lee blindfold" is a remark attributed to Jackson. Now all was over. "Could I have directed events," wrote Lee, ascribing the glory to his stricken comrade, "I should have chosen for the good of the country to be disabled in your stead." Jackson lingered for a week. His arm was amputated. Pneumonia supervened. On the 10th he was told to prepare for death, to which he consented with surprise and fortitude. "Very good, very good; it is all right." Finally, after some hours, quietly and clearly: "Let us cross over the river and rest under the shade of the trees." His loss was a mortal blow to Lee and to the cause of the South.

*   *   *   *   *

Nevertheless in these months the scales of war seemed to turn against the Union. A wave of discouragement swept across the North. Desertion was rife in the Federal ranks. Conscription, called "the draft," was violently resisted in many states. Many troops had to be withdrawn from the front to enforce the law. Many hundreds of lives were lost in New York City in the draft riots. Clement L. Vallandigham, the leader of the peace party, or "Copperheads" as they were called, after a particularly poisonous snake, declared in Congress, "You have not conquered the South; you never will. Money you have expended without limit, blood poured out like water. . . . Defeat, death, taxation, and sepulchres . . . these are your only trophies." The legislatures of Indiana and Illinois threatened to acknowledge the Confederacy. "Everybody feels," wrote Medill, the editor of the *Chicago Tribune,* and a close friend of the President's, "that the war is drawing to a disastrous and disgraceful termination. Money cannot be supplied much longer to a beaten democracy and homesick army." It was indeed the darkest hour. But the heart of Lincoln did not fail him.

Problems on the seas and across the ocean also perplexed and agitated the North. The small Confederate Navy was active and successful in the Gulf of Mexico and on the Atlantic coast. On the high seas Confederate commerce-raiders, built in Britain, were taking a heavy toll of Northern shipping. The most famous of them, the *Alabama,* had stolen out of the river Mersey in June 1862. She sailed under a false name, and in spite of the protests of the American Minister in London. After a glorious career, lasting eleven months, she was brought to bay by a Federal cruiser in the English Channel. A gallant engagement was fought off Cherbourg. It was witnessed by a number of French artists, one of whom, Manet, has left a remarkable painting of the scene. The *Alabama* was outgunned and sunk. The Federal Government pressed Britain hard for compensation for the damage done by the Southern raiders. Negotiations were long and disputatious. They were not concluded until six years after the end of the war, when Gladstone's Government agreed to pay the United States fifteen million dollars.

Throughout the spring and summer of 1863 anxiety grew in Washington because of the building in the British yard which had launched the *Alabama* of two new ironclad Confederate warships. They were fitted with nine-inch rifled guns and formidable underwater rams, thus combining the offensive merits of the *Merrimac* and the *Monitor*. These ships were known as the Laird rams, after their builders. The American Minister bombarded the Foreign Secretary, Lord John Russell, with demands that the Laird rams must not be allowed to escape as the *Alabama* had done. Russell eventually realised that the construction of such vessels by a neutral would set a bad precedent which might work to Britain's disadvantage in future wars. In September he ordered their seizure. Thus was closed the last of the war-time diplomatic crises between Britain and the Union.

* * * * *

The initiative in the field now passed to Lee, who resolved to carry out his long-planned invasion of Pennsylvania. But Vicksburg, on the Mississippi, was in dire straits, and unless Joseph E. Johnston could be largely reinforced its fall was imminent. A proposal was made to stand on the defensive in Virginia, to send Lee himself with Longstreet's two divisions to the Mississippi, and other troops to Middle Tennessee to defeat the covering forces under Rosecrans south of Nashville and threaten the commercial cities of Louisville and Cincinnati, perhaps forcing Grant to abandon his campaign against Vicksburg. Lee refused point-blank to go.

Squarely he put the issue before the Council of War: the risk had to be taken of losing Mississippi or Virginia. His view prevailed, and on May 26, three weeks after Chancellorsville, the invasion of Pennsylvania was sanctioned. The Army of Northern Virginia was reorganised in three corps of three divisions each, commanded by Longstreet, Richard S. Ewell, and A. P. Hill. Lee's object in 1863, as in the previous year, was to force the Army of the Potomac to fight under conditions in which defeat would spell annihilation. In this he saw the sole hope of winning Southern independence.

The movement commenced on June 3. Longstreet concentrated his corps at Culpeper, and behind it the other two corps passed into the Shenandoah valley, marching straight for the Potomac. Longstreet meanwhile moved up on the east of the Blue Ridge with his front and flank screened by Stuart's cavalry, eventually entering the valley behind the other two corps through the northern "Gaps." On the 9th, before the movement was well under way, there was an indecisive cavalry battle at Brandy Station, in which the Federal cavalry, under their new commander, Alfred Pleasanton, regained their morale.

At first the campaign went well for Lee. Ewell on the 10th left Culpeper for the valley, and, marching with a speed worthy of "Stonewall" Jackson, cleared the Federal garrisons out of Winchester and Martinsburg, capturing four thousand prisoners and twenty-eight guns, and on the 15th was crossing the Potomac. He established his corps at Hagerstown, where it waited for a week, till the corps in the rear was ready to cross, and his cavalry brigade pushed on to Chambersburg, in Pennsylvania, to collect and send back supplies. On the 22nd he was ordered to advance farther into Pennsylvania and capture Harrisburg, a hundred miles north of Washington, if it "came within his means."

On the 27th Ewell reached Carlisle, and his outposts next day were within four miles of Harrisburg. The other two Confederate corps were at Chambersburg. As far as Chambersburg Lee had been following the Cumberland valley, with his right flank shielded by the South Mountain range, and as yet he knew nothing of Hooker's movements. He accepted Stuart's plan of making a raid through the mountains and joining Ewell in Pennsylvania. Stuart, who started on the 25th, believed that Hooker was still in his encampments on the east side of the mountains, and expected to be able to ride through his camp areas and cross the Potomac near Leesburg. But Hooker had broken up his camps and was marching that same morning for the Potomac. Stuart had to make a third ride round the Federal rear, crossed the Potomac within twenty miles of Washington, failed to make contact with Ewell's right division, and only rejoined Lee with his men and horses utterly exhausted on the afternoon of July 2. Thus for a whole week Lee had been deprived of the "eyes" of his army; and much had happened meanwhile.

As soon as Lee began his movement to the north Hooker proposed to march on Richmond. But Lincoln forbade him, and rightly pointed out that not Richmond but Lee's army was his proper objective. In thus deciding the President did what Lee had expected. After crossing the Potomac Hooker made his headquarters near Frederick, where he covered Washington and threatened Lee's line of communications. Halleck and Stanton had agreed after Chancellorsville that Hooker must not be in command of the army in the next battle. When therefore the General, denied the use of the Harpers Ferry garrison, tendered his resignation it was promptly accepted. Early in the morning of June 28 General George G. Meade, commander of the Fifth Corps, who was now appointed to the chief command, decided to move his whole army by forced marches northwards to the Susquehanna to prevent Lee from crossing that river, and at the same time to cover Baltimore and Washington. Meade was a safe, dogged commander, with no political affiliations. He could be relied upon to avoid acts of folly, and also anything brilliant. Expecting that Lee would come south from the Susquehanna to attack Baltimore, he now prepared to meet him on the line of Pipe Creek, ten miles beyond Westminster.

Lee had been greatly perplexed by Stuart's failure to report, but, having implicit confidence in him, had concluded that Hooker must still be south of the Potomac. On learning the truth during the 28th he ordered a concentration at Cashtown, close to the eastern foot of South Mountain. He did not hurry, and "the march was conducted with a view to the comfort of the troops." At the outset of the campaign he had been in agreement with Longstreet that the strategy should be offensive and the tactics defensive, and he had no intention of fighting a battle except under favourable conditions. But chance ruled otherwise.

On June 30 a brigade of Hill's corps advanced eight miles from Cashtown to Gettysburg, partly to look for shoes, partly to reconnoitre a place through which Ewell's corps might be moving next day. Gettysburg was found in the hands of some Federal cavalry, which had just entered. The Confederate brigade thereupon turned back without ascertaining the strength of the hostile force. Buford, the Federal cavalry commander, who bore the Christian names of Napoleon B., seems to have been the first man in either army to appreciate the strategical importance of Gettysburg, the meeting-place of some dozen roads from all points of the compass. He moved his division to the west of the town, where he found a strong position behind a stream, and called upon the commander of the First Corps to come to his aid with all speed. The First Corps was followed by the Eleventh Corps.

On July 1 severe fighting began with the leading Confederate troops, and presently Ewell, coming down from the north-east, struck in upon the Federal flank, driving the Eleventh Corps through Gettysburg to seek shelter on higher ground three miles southwards, well named Cemetery Ridge. On this first day of battle fifty thousand men had been engaged, and four Confederate divisions had defeated and seriously injured two Federal corps. It now became a race between Lee and Meade, who could concentrate his forces first. Neither Lee nor Meade wished to fight decisively at this moment or on this ground; but they were both drawn into the greatest and bloodiest battle of the Civil War. Lee could not extricate himself and his supply trains without fighting Meade's army to a standstill, and Meade was equally committed to a field he thought ill-chosen.

Lee wished to open the second day of the battle with an attack by Ewell and Hill on Cemetery Ridge, which he rightly regarded as the key to the Federal position. He was deterred by their objections. Longstreet, when he arrived, argued at length for a manœuvre round Meade's left to place Lee's army between Meade and Washington. Such a movement in the absence of Stuart's cavalry would certainly have been reckless, and it is not easy to see how Lee could have provisioned his army in such a position. Finally Lee formally ordered Longstreet to attack the Federal left at dawn. Longstreet, who entirely disapproved of the rôle assigned to him, did not come into action till four in the afternoon. While he waited for an additional brigade two corps joined the Union Army. Lee, who imagined that the Federal left rested upon the Emmetsburg road, expected that Longstreet's advance

Harrisburg

Carlisle

Susquehanna R.

PENNSYLVANIA

Chambersburg •

• Cashtown

• Gettysburg

M
A
R
Y
L
A
N
D

Potomac R.

• Hagerstown

Westminster •

Martinsburg •

W.   VIRGINIA

• Sharpsburg

• Frederick Town

Harpers Ferry

Baltimore •

Potomac R.

Winchester •

Leesburg •

Washington •

B
L
U
E

R
I
D
G
E

Shenandoah R.

Alexandria •

Manassas Junction •

VIRGINIA

• Brandy Station

Aquia Creek

Rapidan R.

• Fredericksburg

Spotsylvania •

Gordonsville •

Miles

0   10   20   30   40   50

THE
GETTYSBURG
CAMPAIGN

up this road would roll up the Federal line from left to right. But at this point the Federal corps commander, Sickles, had taken up an advanced position on his own authority, and his flank was not the end of the Federal line. When this was discovered Longstreet obstinately refused to depart from the strict letter of his orders, though he knew that Lee was not aware of the true position. All that he achieved after several hours' fierce fighting was to force Sickles back to Meade's main line. On this day the greater part of Hill's corps took no part in the battle. Ewell, who was to have attacked the north end of the ridge as soon as he heard Longstreet's guns, did not get into action till 6 P.M. There were no signs of any co-ordination of attacks on the Confederate side on July 2. Although Lee had failed to make his will prevail, and the Confederate attacks had been unconnected, the losses of the Federal Army were terrible, and Meade at the Council of War that night was narrowly dissuaded from ordering a general retreat.

The third day began. Lee still bid high for victory. He resolved to launch fifteen thousand men, sustained by the fire of a hundred and twenty-five guns, against Meade's left centre, at the point where one of Hill's brigades had pierced the day before. Ewell's corps would at the same time attack from the north, and if the assault under General George E. Pickett broke the Federal line the whole Confederate Army would fall on. Again the attack was ordered for the earliest possible hour. It was the Federals however who opened the third day by recapturing in the grey of the dawn some of the trenches vacated the previous evening, and after hard fighting drove the Confederates before noon entirely off Culp's Hill. Exhausted by this, Ewell made no further movement. Longstreet was still arguing vehemently in favour of a wide turning movement round Meade's left. The heavy losses which his corps had suffered on the 2nd made this more difficult than ever.

The morning passed in utter silence. It was not till one in the afternoon that the Confederates began the heaviest bombardment yet known. Longstreet, unable to rally himself to a plan he deemed disastrous, left it to the artillery commander, Alexander, to give the signal to Pickett. At half-past two the Confederate ammunition, dragged all the way from Richmond in tented wagons, was running short. "Come quick," Alexander said to Pickett, "or my ammunition will not support you properly." "General," said Pickett to Longstreet, who stood sombre and mute, "shall I advance?" By an intense effort Longstreet bowed his head in assent. Pickett saluted and set forty-two regiments against the Union centre. We see to-day, upon this battlefield so piously preserved by North and South, and where many of the guns still stand in their firing stations, the bare, slight slopes up which this grand infantry charge was made. In splendid array, all their battle flags flying, the forlorn assault marched on. But, like the Old Guard on the evening of Waterloo, they faced odds and metal beyond the virtue of mortals. The Federal rifled artillery paused till they were within seven hundred yards; then they opened again with a roar and cut lanes in the steadfastly advancing ranks. On they went, without flinching or disorder; then the deadly sound, like tearing paper, as Lee once described it, rose under and presently above the cannonade. But Pickett's division still drove forward, and at trench, stone wall, or rail fence closed with far larger numbers of men, who, if not so lively as themselves, were at least ready to die for their cause. All three brigadiers in Pickett's division fell killed or mortally wounded. General L. A. Armistead with a few hundred men actually entered the Union centre, and the spot where he died with his hand on a captured cannon is to-day revered by the manhood of the United States.

But where were the reserves to carry through this superb effort? Where were the simultaneous attacks to grip and rock the entire front? Lee at Gettysburg no more than Napoleon at Waterloo could win dominance. The victorious stormers were killed or captured; the rest walked home across the corpses which encumbered the plain amid a remorseless artillery fire. Less than a third came back. Lee met them on his horse Traveller with the only explanation, which they would not accept, "It is all my fault." Longstreet, in memoirs written long afterwards, has left on record a sentence which is his best defence: "As I rode back to the line of batteries, expecting an immediate counter-stroke, the shot and shell ploughed the ground around my horse, and an involuntary appeal went up that one of them would remove me from scenes of such awful responsibility."

But there was no counter-stroke. The Battle of Gettysburg was at an end. Twenty-three thousand Federals and over twenty thousand Confederates had been smitten by lead or steel. As after the Antietam, Lee confronted his foe on the morrow and offered to fight again. But no one knew better that it was decisive. With every personal resource he gathered up his army. An immense wagon train of wounded were jolted, springless, over sixteen miles of crumpled road. "Carry me back to old Virginia." "For God's sake kill me." On the night of the 4th Lee began his retreat. Meade let him go. The energy for pursuit had been expended in the battle. The Potomac was found in flood; Lee's pontoon bridge had been partially destroyed by a raid from the city of Frederick. For a week the Confederates stood at bay behind entrenchments with their backs to an unfordable river. Longstreet would have stayed to court attack; but Lee measured the event. Meade did not appear till the 12th, and his attack was planned for the 14th. When that morning came, Lee, after a cruel night march, was safe on the other side of the river. He carried with him his wounded and his prisoners. He had lost only two guns, and the war.

The Washington Government were extremely discontented with Meade's inactivity; and not without reason. Napoleon might have made Lee's final attack, but he certainly would not have made Meade's impotent pursuit. Lincoln promoted Meade only to the rank of Major-General for his good service at Gettysburg. Lee wended his way back by the Shenandoah valley to his old stations behind the Rappahannock and the Rapidan. The South had shot its bolt.

Up to a certain point the Gettysburg campaign was admirably conducted by Lee, and some of its objects were achieved; but the defeat with which it ended far more than counterbalanced these. The irreparable loss of twenty-eight thousand men in the whole operation out of an army of seventy-five thousand forbade any further attempts to win Southern independence by a victory on Northern soil. Lee believed that his own army was invincible, and after Chancellorsville he had begun to regard the Army of the Potomac almost with contempt. He failed to distinguish between bad troops and good troops badly led. It was not the army but its commander that had been beaten on the Rappahannock. It may well be that had Hooker been allowed to retain his command Lee might have defeated him a second time. Fortune, which had befriended him at Chancellorsville, now turned against him. Stuart's long absence left him blind as to the enemy's movements at the most critical stage of the campaign, and it was during his absence that he made the fatal mistake of moving to the east side of the mountains. Lee's military genius did not shine. He was disconcerted by

Stuart's silence, he was "off his balance," and his subordinates became conscious of this mood. Above all he had not Jackson at his side. Longstreet's recalcitrance had ruined all chance of success at Gettysburg. On Longstreet the South laid the heavy blame.

There was no other battle in the East in 1863, and the armies were left for the winter facing each other on the Rapidan.

*   *   *   *   *

We must now turn to the West, where great battles were fought, and many fell. But since a decisive victory by Lee's army would have enabled him to march where he pleased, and to hold New York and every great city of the Atlantic coast to ransom or surrender, this secondary though spacious theatre need not be precisely lighted. From the West, it is true, the eventual thrust came which split and devastated the South. But its importance in 1862 and 1863 lay chiefly in the advance of Grant to the supreme unified command of the Union armies. The objective was the clearance or barrage of the Mississippi. In April 1862 Admiral Farragut, a Southerner, who adhered to the Union, had become prominent at the head of the Federal Navy. In April, with a fleet of all kinds of vessels, partly armoured or naked, he had run past the forts guarding the approaches to New Orleans, the largest city and the commercial capital of the Confederacy, which fell next day. He had then continued the ascent of the river, and reached Vicksburg on May 18. Finding no Federal troops at hand to support him, he retired to run the batteries again on June 25, and join hands with the Federal flotilla at Memphis. It was therefore known by the end of 1862 that the Confederate batteries could not stop the Union ships. As for the torpedoes, a new word, of which there was then much talk, Farragut was to say, "Damn the torpedoes!"

and be justified. Thenceforward the Union flotillas could move up and down the great river, through its entire course, by paying a toll. This was a substantial aid to the Federal Army on either bank. Here in the Mississippi valley was almost a separate war. The Western states of the Confederacy claimed a great measure of autonomy from Jefferson Davis and his Government at Richmond, while clamouring for its help. At Washington the Western theatre was viewed in much the same way as was the Eastern front by the Allied and associated Powers in the First World War. It was secondary, but also indispensable. It was not the path to victory, but unless it was pursued victory would be long delayed.

After the failure of the river expedition in December 1862 Grant reassembled his army on the right bank of the Mississippi. Vicksburg was still his first aim, but the floods of the Yazoo basin prevented at this season all operations except by water. Having by numerous feints deceived the Confederate General, Pemberton, who with a field army was defending Vicksburg, Grant successfully ferried forty-five thousand men across the Mississippi below the Grand Gulf batteries thirty-six miles down-stream from Vicksburg. He surprised and drove back Pemberton's troops, and on May 3 established himself at Grand Gulf, in a safe position on the uplands, with his left flank protected by the wide Black River, and in touch with the Federal flotillas. Here he was joined four days later by his third corps, under Sherman. He now began a cautious movement towards Vicksburg and the railway which joined it to the town of Jackson. General Joseph E. Johnston, reinforced too late by President Davis, was hurried, ill though he was, to the scene. His only thought now was to extricate Pemberton's army. He ordered that General to march at once to join him before Grant could interpose his three corps between them. Pemberton resolved to disobey this order. He conceived that a movement across Grant's communications with Grand Gulf would compel a Federal retreat. He not only disobeyed, he miscalculated; for Grant, like McClellan before Richmond in 1862, with his command of the rivers, was not dependent upon any one particular base. Dropping his links with Grand Gulf, he pressed Johnston back with his right hand, and then turned on Pemberton in great superiority. After a considerable battle at Champion's Hill, in which over six thousand men fell, Pemberton was driven back into Vicksburg. With the aid of the flotilla the Union General opened a new base north of the city, and after two attempts to storm its defences, one of which cost him four thousand men, commenced a regular siege. Large reinforcements presently raised his army to over seventy thousand men. Johnston, with twenty-four thousand, could do nothing to relieve Pemberton. Vicksburg was starved into surrender, and its Confederate garrison and field army, more than thirty thousand strong, capitulated on July 4, at the very moment of Lee's defeat at Gettysburg. Five days later Port Hudson, in Louisiana, also reduced by famine, surrendered with seven thousand men to General Banks, and the whole course of the Mississippi was at last in Federal hands. "The Father of Waters," said Lincoln, "again goes unvexed to the sea." These were stunning blows to the South.

*　*　*　*　*

The main fury of the war was now transferred to the West. Until the fall of Vicksburg was certain the highly competent Rosecrans, with about sixty thousand men, forming the Union Army of the Cumberland, was content from the scene of his success at Murfreesboro to watch Bragg, who stood across the railway line between him and Chattanooga. This city and railway centre, protected by the deep and wide Tennessee

THE UNION ARMY BEFORE PETERSBURG

Some of the 140,000 men who, under Grant's command, laid siege to Richmond

GENERAL WILLIAM T. SHERMAN

" 'War is hell,' he said, and certainly he made it so."

"cruelty"

ATLANTA, NOVEMBER 1864
Sherman prepares for his march to the sea

SAVANNAH

The town at the end of Sherman's march through Georgia to the sea, captured by Sherman on December 22, 1864

RICHMOND

The capital of the Confedèracy, captured by Federal troops on
April 3, 1865, with (*below*) the ruins of the armoury and, in the
middle ground, the pillars of the Petersburg and Richmond railway
bridge

THE APPOMATTOX COURT HOUSE

Where General Robert E. Lee surrendered to General Ulysses S. Grant on April 9, 1865

THE GRAND REVIEW

With flags on the buildings draped in black and flying at half-mast for the assassinated President, the Grand Army of the Union marched triumphantly through Washington on May 23 and 24, 1865

THE
MISSISSIPPI
THEATRE

River on the north and the high ridges of the Appalachian Mountains, a western chain of the Alleghenies, on the south, was the key not only to the mastery of the Mississippi valley, but to the invasion of prosperous, powerful, and hitherto inviolate Georgia. The waiting period was marked by fierce Confederate cavalry raids to break up the railways behind the Union army, and by Federal counter-strokes against important ironworks and munitions factories in the southern part of Tennessee. In these the Confederates had the advantage. But when Rosecrans, at the end of June, advanced along the railway to Chattanooga, and Burnside, with another army of forty thousand men, a hundred miles to the east, struck at Knoxville, great and far-reaching operations were afoot. Burnside captured Knoxville, cutting one of the sinew railways of the Confederacy. Rosecrans manœuvred Bragg out of all his defensive lines astride the Nashville–Chattanooga railway, and by September 4 gained Chattanooga without a battle.

Until this moment Rosecrans had shown high strategic skill. He now made the disastrous mistake of supposing that the resolute, agile army in his front was cowed. Bragg, who was one of the worst generals, hated by his lieutenants, and nearly always taking the wrong decision, was none the less a substantial fighter. South of Chattanooga the mountain ridges spread out like the fingers of a hand. Bragg lay quiet at Lafayette with an army now reinforced to sixty thousand men. By September 12 Rosecrans realised the appalling fact that his three corps were spread on a sixty-mile front, and that Bragg lay in their midst three times as strong as any one of them. Bragg, overbearing and ill-served, missed this opportunity, which Lee or Jackson would have made decisive for the whole of the West. Rosecrans recoiled, and concentrated towards Chattanooga; but he was too late, even against

Bragg, to escape a battle on ground and under conditions far from his choice.

At Chickamauga, across the border of Georgia, on September 18 Bragg fell upon his enemy. Longstreet, from Virginia, with two divisions and artillery, had reached him, together with other heavy reinforcements, so that he had the rare fortune for a Confederate General of the weight of numbers behind him. Seventy thousand Confederates attacked fifty-five thousand Federals. The two days' battle was fought with desperate valour on both sides. Bragg tried persistently to turn the Federal left and cut Rosecrans from Chattanooga, but when this wing of the Union Army, commanded by General George H. Thomas, had drawn to its aid troops from the centre and right, Longstreet, with twenty thousand Virginian veterans, assaulted the denuded parts of the Union front, and drove two-thirds of Rosecrans' army, with himself and the corps commanders, except Thomas, in ruin from the field. Longstreet begged Bragg to put all his spare weight behind a left-handed punch; but the Commander-in-Chief was set upon his first idea. He continued to butt into Thomas, who had built overnight breastworks of logs and railway iron in the woodland. Night closed upon a scene of carnage surpassed only by Gettysburg. Thomas, "the rock of Chickamauga," extricated himself and his corps and joined the rest of the Federal Army in Chattanooga.

The casualties in this battle were frightful. Sixteen thousand Federals and over twenty thousand Confederates were killed, wounded, or missing. The Confederates, who had captured forty guns and the battlefield, and who for the moment had broken the enemy's power, had gained the victory. It might have been Ramillies, or Waterloo, or even Tannenberg. It was Malplaquet.

Bragg now blockaded and almost surrounded Rosecrans

and the Army of the Cumberland in Chattanooga. He held the two heights which dominated Lookout Mountain and Missionary Ridge. For a time he barred all supplies by the Tennessee River. In early October it looked as if the Army of the Cumberland would be starved into surrender. Meanwhile the position of Burnside at Knoxville, against whom Longstreet had been sent, appeared no less deadly.

The Washington Government now began to lean heavily upon General Ulysses Grant. His faults and weaknesses were apparent; but so also was his stature. On the Union side, baffled, bewildered, disappointed, weary of bloodshed and expense, Grant now began to loom vast and solid through a red fog. Victory had followed him from Fort Donelson to Vicksburg. Here were large rebel surrenders—troops, cannon, territory. Who else could show the like? On October 16 Grant was given command of the departments of the Ohio, Cumberland, and Tennessee Rivers, with his lieutenant, Sherman, under him at the head of the Army of Tennessee.

Rosecrans was dismissed. He had lost a great battle, and under the Washington administration no General survived defeat. He had however played a distinguished part in the West, and his military record was clean. Long before Chickamauga he had lost favour with Halleck. That poor figure, who stood at the portals of the grim politics of these days, who sought to tell the armies what the politicians wanted and the politicians as much as they could understand of the military needs, showed his measure clearly when in February 1863 he wrote to Grant and Rosecrans that the vacant Major-Generalship would be given to whoever won the first notable success. Grant left his letter unanswered. Rosecrans wrote in stern rebuke that "a patriot and a man of honour should require no additional incentive to make him do his duty." Thus when he tripped he fell on stony ground.

By a series of intricate measures Grant freed the Tennessee

River, stormed both Missionary Ridge and Lookout Mountain, and drove Bragg and the Confederate Army in thorough disorder away from Chattanooga. At the same time he relieved Burnside at Knoxville. The frontiers of the Confederacy rolled southwards in another long lap. Vicksburg had cut it in two along the line of the Mississippi. Chattanooga cut the eastern half again along the range of the Alleghenies. By December 1863 the Confederates were driven back into Georgia, and the whole Mississippi valley was recovered for the Union. All these convulsive events might have taken a different grip if President Davis had made Lee Supreme Commander of the Confederate Army after Chancellorsville, or, better still, in 1862, and if he had devoted his authority and fine qualities wholly to the task of rallying behind the chief General the loyal, indomitable, but woefully particularist energies of the South. By the end of 1863 all illusions had vanished. The South knew they had lost the war, and would be conquered and flattened. It is one of the enduring glories of the American nation that this made no difference to the Confederate resistance. In the North, where success was certain, they could afford to have bitter division. On the beaten side the departure of hope left only the resolve to perish arms in hand. Better the complete destruction of the whole generation and the devastation of their enormous land, better that every farm should be burned, every city bombarded, every fighting man killed, than that history should record that they had yielded. Any man can be trampled down by superior force, and death, in whatever shape it comes, is only death, which comes to all. It might seem incredible when we survey the military consequences of 1863 that the torments of war should have been prolonged through the whole of 1864 and into 1865. "Kill us if you can; destroy all we have," cried the South. "As you will," replied the steadfast majority of the North.

CHAPTER SEVEN

The Victory of the Union

THE Confederacy was defeated, and the last long phase of the war was one of conquest and subjugation. During the winter of the year which had witnessed Chancellorsville and Gettysburg, Vicksburg, Chattanooga, and Chickamauga, there was a pause. The North gathered its overwhelming strength for a sombre task. The war-leadership of President Davis was gravely questioned in the South. He had kept in his own hands not only the enormous business of holding the Confederacy together and managing its political and economic life, but he had exercised an overriding control upon its military operations. He had obdurately pursued a defensive policy and strategy, against odds which nothing but decisive victory in the field could shorten. This had led logically and surely to ruin. Lee and Longstreet were now asked for a general plan for 1864. They proposed that Beauregard, with twenty thousand men drawn from the forts in South Carolina, should be joined to Longstreet's army in East Tennessee, and, invading Kentucky, strike at the Louisville railway, the sole line of supply for the main Federal Army, which was expected to advance southward from Chattanooga against Joseph E. Johnston. Thereafter Johnston and all Confederate forces in the West would unite, fighting such battles as might be necessary, in a northward march towards the Ohio. This, they declared, would rupture all Federal combinations in the West. As for the East, Lee and the Army of Northern Virginia would be answerable. When this great scheme was laid before Davis at a Council of War, Bragg, of all men, pressed an alternative plan, with the result that there was no plan. Johnston must fight as best he could in the West, and Lee would continue to defend Richmond.

On March 9 President Lincoln appointed Ulysses Grant to the command of all the armies of the United States, raising him to the rank of Lieutenant-General. At last on the Northern side there was unity of command, and a general capable of exercising it. Grant's plan was brutal and simple. It was summed up in the word "Attrition." In intense fighting and exchange of lives weight of numbers would prevail. To Meade, who nominally retained the command of the Army of the Potomac, he gave the order, "Wherever Lee goes you will go also." To Sherman, his friend and brother officer, who had risen with him, he confided the command in the West with similar instructions, but with an addition: "To move against Johnston's army, to break it up, and to get into the interior country as far as you can, inflicting all the damage you can against their war resources." If either Johnston or Lee, profiting by interior lines, showed signs of trying to join the other no exertion was to be spared to follow him.

Grant also ordered three secondary operations: an attack, aided by the Navy, upon Mobile, on the Gulf of Mexico; pressure from Fortress Monroe towards Richmond; and the devastation of the Shenandoah valley, the granary of the South, and its oft-used route towards Maryland and Washington. Of these diversions the first two failed, and the Shenandoah plan only succeeded late in the year, when two corps and three cavalry divisions were applied to it under General Philip H. Sheridan.

With the approach of spring Grant, having launched the Union Army, came to grips with Lee on the old battle-grounds of the Rappahannock and the Rapidan, where the traces of Chancellorsville remained and memories of "Stonewall" Jackson brooded. He took the field at the beginning of May with a hundred and twenty thousand men against Lee with sixty thousand. He crossed the Rapidan by the fords which "Fighting Joe" Hooker had used the year before. There in the savage country of the Wilderness was fought a battle worthy of its field. In two days of intricate and ferocious fighting, May 5 and 6, Grant was repulsed with a loss of eighteen thousand men, Lee himself losing about ten thousand, the most part in a vehement counter-stroke. Grant then passaged to his left, and in a series of confused struggles from the 8th to the 19th sought to cut the Confederates from their line of retreat upon Richmond. This was called the Battle of Spotsylvania Court House, in which the Federal armies suffered another loss of over eighteen thousand men, or double that of their opponents. Undeterred by this slaughter, Grant repeated his movement to the left, and prolonged heavy fighting followed in the wild regions of the South Anna stream and afterwards on the Pamunkey River. Grant, for all the courage of his men, could never turn Lee's right flank, and Lee and his devoted soldiers could never overcome odds of two to one. They could only inflict death and wounds in proportion to their numbers. According to Grant's war-thought, this process, though costly, had only to be continued long enough to procure the desired result. "I propose to fight it out on this line," he wrote to Halleck at Washington, "if it takes all summer." But other factors, less arithmetical in their character, imposed themselves.

At Cold Harbour, on the ground of the "Seven Days" in 1862, the Federal Commander-in-Chief hurled his army through the blasted, undulating woodland against the haggard, half-starved, but elated Confederate lines. It was at this battle that Lee conversed with the Postmaster-General of the Confederacy, who had ridden out to see the fighting, and asked, "If he breaks your line what reserve have you?" "Not a regiment," said Lee, "and that has been my condition since the fighting commenced. If I shorten my lines to provide a reserve he will turn them; if I weaken my lines to provide a reserve he will break me." But the result of the day ended Grant's tactics of unflinching butchery. After seven thousand brave blue-coated soldiers had fallen in an hour or so the troops refused to renew the assault. More is expected of the high command than determination in thrusting men to their doom. The Union dead and wounded lay between the lines; the dead soon began to stink in the broiling sun, the living screamed for water. But Grant failed to secure a truce for burial and mercy. It was not till the third day after the battle that upon a letter from Lee, saying he would gladly accord it if asked, formal request was made, and for a few hours the firing ceased. During the World Wars through which we have lived no such indulgences were allowed, and numbers dwarfing the scale of the American Civil War perished in "no-man's-land," in long, helpless agony where they fell. But in that comparatively civilised and refined epoch in America Cold Harbour was deemed a horror almost beyond words.

The Army of Northern Virginia had inflicted upon Grant in thirty days a loss equal to its own total strength. He now saw himself compelled to resort to manœuvre. He did exactly what McClellan had done on this same ground two years earlier. By a skilful and daring march, which Lee was too weak to interrupt, he moved his whole army across the peninsula, and, again using sea-power, crossed the James River and established a new base on the south bank. He set himself to attack Richmond by the "back-door," as McClellan had wished to do. Repulsed at Petersburg, he laid siege with an army now reinforced to a hundred and forty thousand men to the trench lines covering that stronghold and the lines east of Richmond. He failed again to turn Lee's right flank by movements south of the James, and at the end of June resigned himself to trench warfare attack by spade, mine, and cannon. There was no investment, for Lee's western flank remained open. There static conditions lasted till April 1865. These performances, although they eventually gained their purpose, must be regarded as the negation of generalship. They were none the less a deadly form of war.

* * * * *

Meanwhile, in the West, Sherman, who enjoyed a superiority of almost two to one, had begun in May to fight his way south along the railway from Chattanooga to Atlanta, deep in Georgia. He was faced by Joseph E. Johnston, with three strong Confederate corps. A remarkable duel ensued between skilful adversaries. Sherman avoided frontal attacks, and by flanking movements manœuvred Johnston out of one strong position after another. Fierce fighting was continuous on the outpost lines, and in a minor engagement one of Johnston's corps commanders, General Leonidas Polk, was killed by a cannon-shot. Only at Kenesaw Mountain did Sherman assault. He was repulsed with the loss of two thousand five hundred men. But meanwhile the spectacle of this remorseless advance and his unwillingness to force a battle cost Johnston the confidence of Jefferson Davis. At the moment when he had resolved to stand at Peach Tree Creek he was superseded by John B. Hood. The Confederate Army, impatient of long retreats, acclaimed the change; but military opinion has always regarded the removal of Johnston as one of the

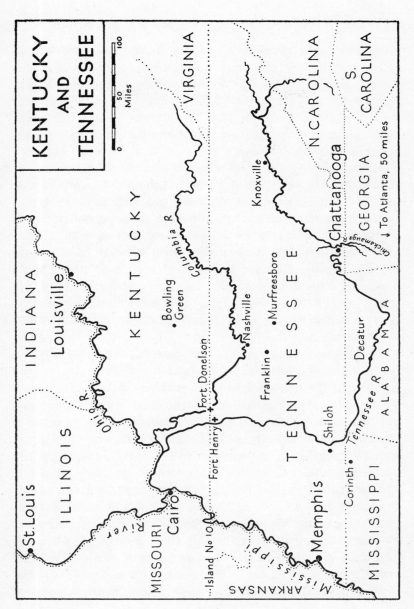

KENTUCKY AND TENNESSEE

worst mistakes of President Davis in his anxious office. Hood felt himself under obligation to attack, and at Peach Tree Creek, Decatur, and East Point he gave full range to the passion for an offensive which inspired the Government he served and the army he led. The Confederates, defending their native soil, hurled themselves against the invader, and suffered irreparable losses. At Decatur alone they lost ten thousand men, without inflicting a third of that loss upon the enemy. After East Point, where five thousand Confederates fell, both the Army of the West and the Richmond Government were convinced that Johnston had probably been right. Hood was directed to return to the defensive, and after some weeks of siege was driven from Atlanta. In the four months' fighting Sherman had carried the Union flag a hundred and fifty miles into the Confederacy, with a loss of thirty-two thousand men. The Confederate loss exceeded thirty-five thousand. Thus Sherman could claim a solid achievement.

This victory prepared another. Indeed, the most important conflict of 1864 was fought with votes. It was astonishing that in the height of ruthless civil war all the process of election should be rigidly maintained. Lincoln's first term was expiring, and he must now submit himself to the popular vote of such parts of the American Union as were under his control. Nothing shows the strength of the institutions which he defended better than this incongruous episode. General McClellan, whom he had used hardly, was the Democratic candidate. His platform at Chicago in August was "that after four years of failure to restore the Union by the experiment of war . . . immediate efforts be made for the cessation of hostilities . . . and peace be restored on the basis of a Federal Union of the states." This proposal was known as the Peace Plank. Republicans had no difficulty in denouncing it

as disloyal. In fact it represented the views of only a section
of the Democrats. The worst that can be said about it is that
it was absurd. All knew that the South would never consent
to the restoration of the Federal Union while life and strength
remained. In Lincoln's own Cabinet Salmon P. Chase, Secretary of the Treasury, a man of proved ability, became his
rival for the Republican nomination. This was one of a number of moves made by Republican malcontents to displace
their leader by someone whom they imagined would be a
more vigorous President. Lincoln's political foes, gazing
upon him, did not know vigour when they saw it. These
were hard conditions under which to wage a war to the death.
The awful slaughters to which Grant had led the Army of
the Potomac and the prolonged stalemate outside Richmond
made a sinister impression upon the North. But the capture
of Atlanta, and a descent by Admiral Farragut upon the
harbour of Mobile, the last Confederate open port, both gave
that surge of encouragement which party men know how to
use. Four million citizens voted in November 1864, and Lincoln was chosen by a majority of only four hundred thousand. Narrow indeed was the margin of mass support by
which his policy of the remorseless coercion of the Southern
states to reincorporation was carried. This did not mean that
all Democrats wanted peace at any price. McClellan had
made it plain when he accepted nomination that the South
must offer to return to the Union before an armistice could
be negotiated. But the founders of the American Constitution, which was now based upon the widest male suffrage,
had so devised the machinery that the choice of the President should be indirect; and in the electoral college Lincoln,
who carried every Union state except New Jersey, Delaware,
and Kentucky, commanded two hundred and twelve delegates against only twenty-one.

In order to placate or confuse the pacifist vote Lincoln had encouraged unofficial peace parleys with the South. Horace Greeley, of the *New York Tribune,* was the President's representative. He met the Southern emissaries in Canada at Niagara Falls. Greeley soon discovered that they had no authority to negotiate a peace. The move would in any case have failed, since Lincoln's conditions now included the abolition of slavery as well as Reunion. The fourth winter of this relentless moral and physical struggle between communities who now respected and armies who had long admired one another came on.

Although Atlanta had fallen Hood's army of forty-four thousand bitter men was still active in the field and free to strike at Sherman's communications. With him were also ten thousand cavalry under Nathan B. Forrest, a new figure who gleamed in the sunset of the Confederacy. Forrest could hardly read or write, but by general account he possessed military qualities of the highest order. His remark that the art of war consists of being "Firstest with mostest" is classic. All these forces were at large around and behind Sherman. On November 12 that General, having persuaded a naturally anxious Washington Cabinet, cast his communications to the winds and began his grim march through Georgia to the shores of the Atlantic. When the Northern blockade had practically stopped the export of cotton from the Confederacy the women, with the slaves, who obeyed and respected them, had sowed the fields with corn. Georgia was full of food in this dark winter. Sherman set himself to march through it on a wide front, living on the country, devouring and destroying all farms, villages, towns, railroads, and public works which lay within his wide-ranging reach. He left behind him a blackened trail, and hatreds which pursue his memory to this day. "War is hell," he said, and certainly he made it so.

But no one must suppose that his depredations and pillage were comparable to the atrocities which were committed during the World Wars of the twentieth century or to the barbarities of the Middle Ages. Searching investigation has discovered hardly a case of murder or rape. None the less a dark shadow lies upon this part of the map of the United States.

Meanwhile Hood, with the Confederate Army of the West, not only tore up Sherman's communications with the United States, so that he was not heard of for a month, but with an army of nearly sixty thousand men struck deep into the Northern conquests. He invaded Tennessee, Thomas, who had been left by Sherman to watch him, retiring. His soldiers, infuriated by the tales of what was happening in their homes, drove the Federals from Franklin, though at the cost of nearly seven thousand men. It looked as if the Confederates might once more break through to the Ohio. But, pressing on, they were defeated and routed by Thomas on December 15 in the Battle of Nashville. Hood returned in much disorder to the South. Sherman, after vicissitudes, reached Savannah on the ocean coast in time to send the news of its fall as a "Christmas present" to the re-established President Lincoln.

* * * * *

The end was now in sight. Sherman planned for 1865 a more severe punishment for South Carolina than had been inflicted upon Georgia. Here was a state which by its arrogance had let loose these years of woe upon the American people. Here were the men who had fired upon the Stars and Stripes at Fort Sumter. In Lincoln's Cabinet Ministers spoke of obliterating Charleston and sowing the foundations with salt. Sherman marched accordingly with extreme vigour. But meanwhile outside Richmond Lee's powers of resistance were exhausted. He had not been deterred by Grant's arrival on the south bank of the James from sending General Early with a strong detachment into the Shenandoah valley. In July 1864 Early defeated the Federal commanders in the Jackson style, and once again Washington had heard the cannon of an advancing foe. But now the Shenandoah had been cleared and devastated by Sheridan with overwhelming forces. The Petersburg lines before Richmond had long repelled every Federal assault. The explosion of a gigantic mine under the defences had only led to a struggle in the crater, in which four thousand Northerners fell. But the weight which lay upon Lee could no longer be borne.

It was not until the beginning of February 1865, in this desperate strait, that President Davis appointed him Commander-in-Chief. In the same month another attempt was made at negotiation. The Vice-President of the Confederacy, A. H. Stephens, was empowered to meet the President of the United States on board a steamer in Hampton Roads, at the mouth of the James River. It offers a strange spectacle, which has not been repeated since, that two opposed belligerent leaders should thus parley in the midst of war. Moreover, the Southern representative had not so many years ago been an acquaintance of Lincoln's. But neither side had the slightest intention of giving way on the main issue. Jefferson Davis in his instructions spoke of a treaty "whereby our two countries may dwell in peace together." Lincoln offered a wide generosity, but only if the United States were again to be one country. It was as he had predicted. The South could not voluntarily re-accept the Union. The North could not voluntarily yield it.

Lee meanwhile had at once restored Joseph E. Johnston to the command of the Western Army. No rule can be laid down upon the High Command of states and armies in war. All depends upon the facts and the men. But should a great general appear the civil Government would be wise to give him full scope at once in the military sphere. After the Second

Manassas, or after Chancellorsville at the latest, Lee was plainly discernible as the Captain-General of the South. But that was in the spring of '62; it was now the spring of '65. Every Confederate counter-offensive had been crushed. The forces of the North ravaged the doomed Confederacy, and at last Grant closed upon its stubborn capital.

On Sunday, April 2, after the Battle of Five Forks and the turning of the Petersburg lines, President Davis sat in his pew in the church at Richmond. A messenger came up the aisle. "General Lee requests immediate evacuation." Southward then must the Confederate Government wander. There were still some hundreds of miles in which they exercised authority. Nothing crumbled, no one deserted; all had to be overpowered, man by man and yard by yard. Lee had still a plan. He would march swiftly south from Richmond, unite with Johnston, break Sherman, and then turn again to meet Grant and the immense Army of the Potomac. But all this was for honour, and mercifully that final agony was spared. Lee, disengaging himself from Richmond, was pursued by more than three times his numbers, and Sheridan, with a cavalry corps, lapped around his line of retreat and broke in upon his trains. When there were no more half-rations of green corn and roots to give to the soldiers, and they were beset on three sides, Grant ventured to appeal to Lee to recognise that his position was hopeless. Lee bowed to physical necessity. He rode on Traveller to Appomattox Court House to learn what terms would be offered. Grant wrote them out in a few sentences. The officers and men of the Army of Northern Virginia must surrender their arms and return on parole to their homes, not to be molested while they observed the laws of the United States. Lee's officers were to keep their swords. Food would be provided from the Union wagons. Grant added, "Your men must keep their horses and mules. They will need them for the spring ploughing." This was the greatest day in the career of General Grant, and stands high in the story of the United States. The Army of Northern Virginia, which so long had "carried the Confederacy on its bayonets," surrendered, twenty-seven thousand strong; and a fortnight later, despite the protests of President Davis, Johnston accepted from Sherman terms similar to those granted to Lee. Davis himself was captured by a cavalry squadron. The armed resistance of the Southern states was thus entirely subdued.

Lincoln had entered Richmond with Grant, and on his return to Washington learned of Lee's surrender. Conqueror and master, he towered above all others, and four years of assured power seemed to lie before him. By his constancy under many varied strains and amid problems to which his training gave him no key he had saved the Union with steel and flame. His thoughts were bent upon healing his country's wounds. For this he possessed all the qualities of spirit and wisdom, and wielded besides incomparable authority. To those who spoke of hanging Jefferson Davis he replied, "Judge not that ye be not judged." On April 11 he proclaimed the need of a broad and generous temper and urged the conciliation of the vanquished. At Cabinet on the 14th he spoke of Lee and other Confederate leaders with kindness, and pointed to the paths of forgiveness and goodwill. But that very night as he sat in his box at Ford's Theatre a fanatical actor, one of a murder gang, stole in from behind and shot him through the head. The miscreant leapt on the stage, exclaiming, *"Sic semper tyrannis,"* and although his ankle was broken through his spur catching in an American flag he managed to escape to Virginia, where he was hunted down and shot to death in a barn. Seward, Secretary of State, was also stabbed at his home, though not fatally, as part of the same plot.

Lincoln died next day, without regaining consciousness, and with him vanished the only protector of the prostrate South. Others might try to emulate his magnanimity; none but he could control the bitter political hatreds which were rife. The assassin's bullet had wrought more evil to the United States than all the Confederate cannonade. Even in their fury the Northerners made no reprisals upon the Southern chiefs. Jefferson Davis and a few others were, indeed, confined in fortresses for some time, but afterwards all were suffered to dwell in peace. But the death of Lincoln deprived the Union of the guiding hand which alone could have solved the problems of reconstruction and added to the triumph of armies those lasting victories which are gained over the hearts of men.

> Who overcomes
> By force hath overcome but half his foe.

Thus ended the great American Civil War, which must upon the whole be considered the noblest and least avoidable of all the great mass-conflicts of which till then there was record. Three quarters of a million men had fallen on the battlefield. The North was plunged in debt; the South was ruined. The material advance of the United States was cast back for a spell. The genius of America was impoverished by the alienation of many of the parent elements in the life and history of the Republic. But, as John Bright said to his audience of English working folk, "At last after the smoke of the battlefield had cleared away the horrid shape which had cast its shadow over the whole continent had vanished and was gone for ever."

INDEX

INDEX

with the *Merrimac*, 70-2; in Mississippi, 92, 112; and *Alabama*, 101-2

Five Forks, Battle of, 131

Florida, purchased from Spain, 2; secession of, 34

Floyd, John Buchanan, 36, 55

Force Act, 11

Forrest, General Nathan B., 128

Fort Donelson, Tennessee, 54, 55

Fort Henry, Tennessee, 54, 55

Fort Sumter, South Carolina, 36, 38, 129

Fortress Monroe, Virginia, 70, 121; landings at, 57, 61; embarkation of McClellan's army at, 75

France, slave trade of, 20-1

Franklin, Kentucky, 129

Frayser's Farm, Battle of, 68

Frederick, Maryland, 80, 104

Fredericksburg, 64; Battle of, 90-91; Sedgwick at, 94-8

Frémont, General John C., 56, 64

Fugitive Slave Law, 27; Northern defiance of, 29, 32, 33

Gaines's Mill, Battle of, 67

Garrison, William Lloyd, 14, 23

Georgia, secession of, 34; fighting in, 117, 124; Confederates driven back into, 119; Sherman devastates, 128-9

Gettysburg, Battle of, 105-11

Glendale, Battle of, 68

Gold, in U. S., 16

Gordonsville, Virginia, 74, 88

Grand Gulf, Mississippi, 113-14

Grant, General Ulysses S., in Mexican War, 15-16; seizes Fort Henry and Fort Donelson, 55; at Shiloh, 60; attacks Vicksburg, 91-2, 102, 113-14; given

command in West, 118; given complete command, 121; plan of, 121; campaign of, against Lee, 121-24; ruthlessness of, 123; takes Richmond, 131-32; Lee surrenders to, 131

Great Lakes, disarmament on, 1

Great Plains, cultivation of, 27; free soil and slavery in, 28-31

Greeley, Horace, 86, 128

Grey, Earl, 23

Hagerstown, Maryland, 103

Halleck, General Henry W., caution of, 54, 61; military adviser to Lincoln, 57; in command in West, 60; General-in-Chief, 69; and McClellan, 79; refuses to withdraw garrisons, 80; and Hooker, 104; and Rosecrans, 118

Hamilton, Alexander, 1, 25

Hampton Roads, peace talks in, 130

Harpers Ferry, 57; Brown liberates slaves at, 32; Confederates hold, 47-8; recovered by Federal Army, 48; Jackson captures, 80-2

Harrisburg, Pennsylvania, 103

Harrison's Landing, 67

Hatteras Inlet, 60

Hazel Grove, 98, 99

Henry Hill, Battle of, 49

Hill, General Ambrose P., at Antietam, 83; at Chancellorsville, 94; in invasion of Pennsylvania, 103; at Gettysburg, 105-8; mentioned, 25

Holmes, General Theophilus H., 91

Holy Alliance, 2

INDEX

Hood, General John B., 67; in command in West, 124, 126-29

Hooker, General Joseph, given command, 90, 93; plan of campaign of, 95-6; at Chancellorsville, 96-9, 111; crosses the Potomac, 104; resigns, 104

Houston, General Sam, 14

Illinois, high road to, 6; threatens to acknowledge Confederacy, 101; mentioned, 31

Indiana, threatens to acknowledge Confederacy, 101

Indians, 4, 19

Ironclad ships, 70-3, 102

Island No. 10, 54, 61

Jackson, Andrew, in Florida, 2; Presidency of, 8-9, 12; problems before, 9, 12; refuses to renew Bank charter, 12

Jackson, Mississippi, 113

Jackson, Thomas ("Stonewall"), 40; at Harpers Ferry, 48, 80-1; at Bull Run, 49-50; Shenandoah campaign of, 64-5; fails to reach Lee in time, 66-7; at Glendale, 68; at Cedar Mountain, 74; destroys Pope's supplies, 76; at Antietam, 82-3; in withdrawal, 88; at Fredericksburg, 90; at Chancellorsville, 95-100; death of, 99-100; mentioned, 57

James River, McClellan retreats to, 67-8; blockade of mouth of, 70; *Merrimac* in, 73; Federal forces at mouth of, 94; Grant crosses, 123, 129; mentioned, 47, 57, 94

Jefferson, Thomas, 1, 3, 8; idea of soverign state rights of, 25

Jefferson City, Missouri, 44

Johnston, General Albert Sidney, defeated on Mississippi, 53-5; in supreme command in West, 60; death of, 60-1

Johnston, General Joseph E., at Harpers Ferry, 47-8; at Bull Run, 49; plan for attack on, 56; threatens Washington, 57; retires behind Rapidan, 61; wounded at Seven Pines, 65; in command in West, 91; needs reinforcement, 102; fails before Vicksburg, 114; plan for campaign of, 120-21; campaign against, 121, 124; dismissal of, 124; restored to command, 130; surrender of, 132; mentioned, 25

Kansas, 28; anti-slavery violence in, 29

Kansas-Nebraska Act, 28, 29, 31

Kenesaw Mountain, 124

Kentucky, 3; and state rights, 9; and secession, 37; remains in Union, 43-4, 47; plan to invade, 120

"Kitchen Cabinet," 9

Knoxville, Tennessee, 116-19

Lafayette, Georgia, 116

Laird rams, 102

Lawrence, Kansas, 29

Lee, General FitzHugh, 25

Lee, General Robert E., 39; in Mexican War, 15, 39; against slavery, 25, 39; captures John Brown, 32; in command of Virginian forces, 40; in Western Virginia, 51; sent to organize coast defences, 51, 60; military